1,001 FACTS ABOUT
RUNNING BACKS

Eric Dickerson

Tony Dorsett

1,001 FACTS ABOUT

RUNNING BACKS

Marcus Allen

BY BRIAN PETERSON

DK Publishing, Inc.

LONDON, NEW YORK, MELBOURNE,
MUNICH, AND DELHI

Project Editor Elizabeth Hester
Senior Art Editor Michelle Baxter
Publisher Chuck Lang
Creative Director Tina Vaughan
Production Chris Avgherinos

NFL CREATIVE
Editor-in-Chief John Wiebusch
Managing Editor John Fawaz
Project Art Director Bill Madrid
Director–Manufacturing Dick Falk
Director–Print Services Tina Dahl
Manager–Computer Graphics Sandy Gordon

First American Edition, 2003
2 4 6 8 10 9 7 5 3 1

Published in the United States by DK Publishing, Inc.
375 Hudson Street, New York, New York 10014

A catalog record for this book is available from the Library of Congress.

ISBN: 0-7894-9861-8

DK Publishing books are available at special discounts for bulk purchases for sales promotions or premiums.
Special editions, including personalized covers, excerpts of existing guides, and corporate imprints can be
created in large quantities for specific needs. For more information, contact Special Markets Dept./
DK Publishing, Inc./375 Hudson Street/New York, New York 10014/FAX: 800-600-9098.

Color reproduction by Hong Kong Scanner
Printed in Singapore by Star Standard

Discover more at
www.dk.com

CONTENTS

LEADING MEN 6

SMOOTH OPERATORS 26

ROAD GRADERS 50

SHOW STOPPERS 70

THE NEXT GENERATION 94

STATISTICS 116

LEADING MEN

MARCUS ALLEN

Ht: 6'2" Wt: 210 Pro Career: 1982–1997

Few running backs possessed the combination of power and grace of Marcus Allen, who was equally talented at running or catching the ball and even throwing (he had 6 career touchdown passes) during his 16-year NFL career. From the first time he stepped on the field, he seemed destined for greatness. He starred at USC, winning the 1981 Heisman Trophy. In Super Bowl XVIII, he rushed for a then-record 191 yards, propelling the Los Angeles Raiders to victory over Washington. Allen currently ranks third all time with 145 touchdowns, fifth with 17,654 yards from scrimmage, and seventh with 12,243 rushing yards. He entered the Pro Football Hall of Fame in 2003.

Born: 3/26/60
Hometown: San Diego, CA
College: Southern California
NFL Draft: 1st Round, 1982

Allen Trivia: *Allen played 11 seasons with the Los Angeles Raiders. With what team did he play his final five NFL seasons?*

JIM BROWN

Ht: 6'2" Wt: 232 Pro Career: 1957–1965

Many people rank Jim Brown as the greatest running back, if not the greatest player, of all time. He used an awesome combination of power and speed to lead the league in rushing in eight of his nine seasons with the Cleveland Browns. Even though he cut his NFL career short to become an actor, Brown held 20 records when he retired, including rushing yards for a career (12,312), season (1,863), and game (237). He also set career records for carries, 100-yard games, 200-yard games, 1,000-yard seasons, rushing touchdowns and total touchdowns, and averaged a remarkable 5.22 yards per carry.

Born: *2/17/36*
Hometown: *St. Simons Isl., GA*
College: *Syracuse*
NFL Draft: *1st Round, 1957*

Brown Trivia: *Brown was inducted into the Pro Football Hall of Fame in 1971. In which two seasons was he named the NFL's MVP?*

ERIC DICKERSON

Ht: *6'3"* Wt: *220* Pro Career: *1983–1993*

Following a prolific college career, Eric Dickerson was selected by the Los Angeles Rams with the second pick in the 1983 NFL Draft, and he immediately lived up to expectations. He set NFL rookie records for rushing yards and rushing touchdowns. In 1984, he produced the greatest single season by a running back in league history—rushing for a record 2,105 yards—and finished his Pro Football Hall of Fame career behind only Walter Payton on the all-time rushing list. Fast for his size, Dickerson set a postseason record with 248 rushing yards against Dallas in 1985.

Born: *9/2/60*
Hometown: *Sealy, TX*
College: *Southern Methodist*
NFL Draft: *1st Round, 1983*

Dickerson Trivia: *By what nickname was the running-back combination of Dickerson and Craig James known at Southern Methodist University?*

TONY DORSETT

Ht: 5'11" Wt: 192 Pro Career: 1977–1988

Tony Dorsett finished college as the NCAA's all-time leading rusher and won the 1976 Heisman Trophy, but there were still questions about whether he was big enough to succeed in the NFL. "I was the skinny kid…who wasn't supposed to make it," Dorsett said. He quieted critics by rushing for more than 1,000 yards in his first season, earning rookie-of-the-year honors, and helping the Dallas Cowboys win Super Bowl XII. TD lived up to his nickname by scoring 91 touchdowns during his 12-year NFL career. Elected to the Pro Football Hall of Fame in 1994, Dorsett gained at least 1,000 yards eight times and finished with 12,739 career rushing yards.

Born: 4/7/54
Hometown: Rochester, PA
College: Pittsburgh
NFL Draft: 1st Round, 1977

Dorsett Trivia: *In a victory over the Minnesota Vikings in 1982, Tony set the NFL record for the longest run from scrimmage. How far did he run?*

MARSHALL FAULK

Ht: *5'10"* **Wt:** *208* **Pro Career:** *1994-present*

Marshall Faulk is more than just a running back—he is one of the greatest offensive players in NFL history. Faulk, the second overall pick of the 1994 draft, played five productive seasons with Indianapolis, but he didn't begin rewriting the record book until the Colts traded him to the Rams in 1999. He is the only person to gain more than 2,000 yards from scrimmage in four consecutive seasons (1998–2001), and he set a league record with 2,429 total yards in 1999. Faulk also set an NFL single-season record by scoring 26 touchdowns in 2000, and his career total of 120 touchdowns ranked seventh all time entering 2003.

Born: *2/26/73*
Hometown: *New Orleans, LA*
College: *San Diego State*
NFL Draft: *1st Round, 1994*

Faulk Trivia: *Marshall is one of two players in NFL history to have gained at least 5,000 rushing yards with two teams. Name the other player.*

FRANCO HARRIS

Ht: 6'2" Wt: 230 Pro Career: 1972–1984

The Pittsburgh Steelers would have had a difficult time winning one Super Bowl during the 1970s—much less four—had it not been for Franco Harris. One of the most productive backs in NFL history (12,120 yards), he was especially dominating in the playoffs. Harris holds the postseason record for most carries and trails only Emmitt Smith in rushing yards and touchdowns. Elected to the Pro Football Hall of Fame in 1990, Harris set Steelers records for career yards and 100-yard rushing games. A fan favorite in Pittsburgh, Harris had his own cheering section nicknamed "Franco's Army."

Born: 3/7/50
Hometown: Fort Dix, NJ
College: Penn State
NFL Draft: 1st Round, 1972

Harris Trivia: *In a 1972 divisional playoff victory over the Oakland Raiders, Franco scored the game-winning touchdown on what famous play?*

Answer: The Immaculate Reception

WALTER PAYTON

Ht: 5'10" Wt: 200 Pro Career: 1975–1987

Nicknamed "Sweetness" because of his easygoing personality and athletic grace, Walter Payton was one of the most tenacious competitors in NFL history. His legendary offseason conditioning program helped him become the all-time NCAA scoring leader and surpass Jim Brown as the NFL's all-time leading rusher (16,726 yards). A nine-time Pro Bowl selection who was inducted into the Pro Football Hall of Fame in 1993, Payton wrote his name throughout the NFL record book, setting standards for most 1,000-yard rushing seasons and most combined yards (21,803).

Born: 7/25/54
Hometown: Columbia, MS
College: Jackson State
NFL Draft: 1st Round, 1975

Payton Trivia: *Walter rushed for more than 100 yards in 77 games. Against which team did he set a record with 275 rushing yards?*

BARRY SANDERS

Ht: 5'8" Wt: 203 Pro Career: 1989–1998

Barry Sanders' lightning-quick moves and incredible balance made him one of the game's most electrifying players. He burst onto the scene with the Detroit Lions after winning the 1988 Heisman Trophy. After rushing for more than 1,000 yards in each of his first eight seasons, Sanders gained a career-best 2,053 yards in 1997 and became the only player to rush for more than 2,000 yards in one season in both college and the NFL. He stunned many people when he retired two years later with 15,269 career rushing yards— just 1,457 short of the NFL record then owned by Walter Payton.

Born: 7/16/68
Hometown: Wichita, KS
College: Oklahoma State
NFL Draft: 1st Round, 1989

Sanders Trivia: *Barry, who rushed for more than 150 yards in a record 25 games, shares the same hometown with which other great NFL running back?*

EMMITT SMITH

Ht: 5'9" Wt: 207 Pro Career: 1990–present

Emmitt Smith has been a record breaker at every level, so it was only fitting that he achieved the ultimate honor for a running back in 2002. That's when Smith surpassed Walter Payton (16,726) to become the NFL's all-time leading rusher (Smith finished the year with 17,162 yards). An All-America running back in high school and college, Emmitt overcame a supposed lack of breakaway speed to capture four NFL rushing titles and earn eight Pro Bowl selections during the first 10 years of his NFL career. He also is the all-time leader in rushing touchdowns (153) and holds the season record for rushing touchdowns (25 in 1995).

Born: 5/15/69
Hometown: Pensacola, FL
College: Florida
NFL Draft: 1st Round, 1990

Smith Trivia: *Emmitt helped the Cowboys win three Super Bowls during the 1990s. In which of those Super Bowls was he named most valuable player?*

SMOOTH OPERATORS

TIKI BARBER

Ht: *5'10"* **Wt:** *205* **Pro Career:** *1997–present*

Tiki Barber, the engine that drives the Giants' offense, has been one of the league's most versatile and productive players. In 2000, he helped New York earn a berth in Super Bowl XXXV by leading the team in touchdowns (9) and rushing (1,006 yards), and by catching 70 passes for 719 yards. In 2002, he ran for a career-high 1,387 yards—second most in franchise history—and caught 69 passes. Barber also led the NFC with 1,984 total yards from scrimmage, increasing his career total to 7,344. He is within a season of passing Frank Gifford (9,043) as the club's all-time leader.

Born: *4/7/75*
Hometown: *Roanoke, VA*
College: *Virginia*
NFL Draft: *2nd Round, 1997*

Barber Trivia: *Tiki has an identical twin brother Ronde, who plays for the Tampa Bay Buccaneers. What position does Ronde play?*

Answer: Cornerback

ROGER CRAIG

Ht: 6'0" Wt: 222 Pro Career: 1983–1993

An excellent runner and receiver, Roger Craig proved to be a perfect running back for the West Coast Offense run by the San Francisco 49ers. In 1984, he led the 49ers with 71 receptions and capped that season by scoring a record 3 touchdowns (1 rushing, 2 receiving) in San Francisco's 38–16 victory over Miami in Super Bowl XIX. The following year, Craig led the league with 92 catches and became the first player in NFL history to gain more than 1,000 yards rushing (1,050) and receiving (1,016) in the same season. The four-time Pro Bowl selection finished his career with 8,189 rushing yards and 4,911 receiving yards.

Born: *7/10/60*
Hometown: *Davenport, IA*
College: *Nebraska*
NFL Draft: *2nd Round, 1983*

Craig Trivia: *Roger is best remembered for his eight seasons with the 49ers, but for what other two franchises did he also play?*

TERRELL DAVIS

Ht: 5'11" Wt: 206 Pro Career: 1995–2001

An unheralded college player, Terrell Davis wasn't expected to become one of the NFL's most dominating running backs. But dominate he did, from the start—Davis set a Broncos rookie record with 1,117 rushing yards in 1995. That was the first of four consecutive seasons with more than 1,000 rushing yards, including 2,008 in 1998—the third highest single-season total in NFL history. Davis also scored a club-record 23 touchdowns and was selected the league's MVP in 1998. A year earlier, he ran for 157 yards and 3 scores to earn MVP honors in Super Bowl XXXII, the first of the Broncos' back-to-back NFL championships.

Born: 10/28/72
Hometown: San Diego, CA
College: Georgia
NFL Draft: 6th Round, 1995

Davis Trivia: *Terrell holds or shares 56 Broncos records, including career rushing yards. After which Motown recording star is Terrell named?*

COREY DILLON

Ht: 6'1" Wt: 225 Pro Career: 1997–present

The Cincinnati Bengals try to keep the ball on the ground, which is not surprising considering Corey Dillon is in the Bengals' backfield. In his first six seasons (1997–2002), Dillon became the club's all-time leading rusher (7,520 yards) and established himself as one of the NFL's premier backs. The slashing runner gained more than 1,000 rushing yards in all six seasons and broke one of the league's most coveted rushing records—he gained 278 yards against the Broncos in 2000, surpassing Walter Payton's single-game record of 275. A three-time Pro Bowl selection, Dillon holds 16 Bengals rushing records.

Born: 10/24/74
Hometown: Seattle, WA
College: Washington
NFL Draft: 2nd Round, 1997

Dillon Trivia: *Corey broke an NFL rookie mark with 246 rushing yards in a game against Tennessee. Which legendary running back previously held the mark?*

CHUCK FOREMAN

Ht: 6'2" Wt: 210 Pro Career: 1973–1980

Chuck Foreman, equally adept as a runner or a receiver, was one of the main reasons the Minnesota Vikings won six consecutive division titles and made three Super Bowl appearances from 1973–78. He earned NFL rookie of the year honors in 1973 and went on to rush for 5,950 yards and compile 3,156 receiving yards during an eight-year career. Twice he led the NFL in total touchdowns (1974 and 1976). In 1975, he led the league with 73 receptions, finished second to Jim Otis for the NFC rushing title, and scored 22 touchdowns. He was selected to play in five Pro Bowls.

Born: 10/26/50
Hometown: Frederick, MD
College: Miami
NFL Draft: 1st Round, 1973

Foreman Trivia: *During the 1970s, NFL fans knew all about Chuck Foreman, but Chuck is not his real name. What is it?*

EDDIE GEORGE

Ht: *6'3"* **Wt:** *240* **Pro Career:** *1996–present*

In 2002, Eddie George reached a landmark milestone as he passed Hall of Fame running back Earl Campbell (8,574 yards) to become the Tennessee Titans' career rushing leader. George gained 1,165 yards in 2002, marking his sixth season with more than 1,000 rushing yards and increasing his career total to 8,978. George, who won the Heisman Trophy in 1995 after running for 1,927 yards and 24 touchdowns, is the portrait of durability. His 112 consecutive starts are the third most by any running back in NFL history, surpassed only by Ricky Watters (114) and Walter Payton (170).

Born: *9/24/73*
Hometown: *Philadelphia, PA*
College: *Ohio State*
NFL Draft: *1st Round, 1996*

George Trivia: *What two running backs were selected before Eddie in the 1996 NFL Draft?*

LEROY KELLY

Ht: **6'0"** *Wt:* **202** *Pro Career:* **1964–1973**

When Jim Brown retired after the 1965 season, he left a gaping hole in the Cleveland Browns' backfield. Leroy Kelly was the player who filled it. In fact, the Browns made the playoffs more often with Kelly in the backfield than with Brown. Kelly hadn't received much notice his first two years despite leading the NFL in punt returns in 1965. But in 1966, he finished second in the NFL with 1,147 rushing yards, and then finished first in each of the next two years (1,205 in 1967 and 1,239 in 1968). Kelly ended his Pro Football Hall of Fame career with 7,274 rushing yards and 90 touchdowns.

Born: **5/20/42**
Hometown: **Philadelphia, PA**
College: **Morgan State**
NFL Draft: **8th Round, 1964**

Kelly Trivia: *Leroy was inducted into the Pro Football Hall of Fame in 1994. What latter-day running sensation was inducted the same year?*

CURTIS MARTIN

Ht: 5'11" Wt: 205 Pro Career: 1995–present

Few people predicted that Curtis Martin would become an NFL star after he missed most of his final college season with an ankle injury. But the quiet, unassuming player with deceptive speed has become one of the best running backs in league history after just eight seasons. In 1995, Martin became the first rookie in 12 years to lead the AFC in rushing, and the following season, he made the first of four Pro Bowl appearances. He is only the second player in NFL history to rush for more than 1,000 yards in each of his first eight seasons. He has gained 10,361 yards in his career (entering 2003).

Born: 5/1/73
Hometown: Pittsburgh, PA
College: Pittsburgh
NFL Draft: 3rd Round, 1995

Martin Trivia: *Curtis is the second leading rusher in New York Jets history. With which team did he begin his NFL career?*

ERNIE NEVERS

Ht: 6'0" Wt: 204 Pro Career: 1926–1931

In pro football's early years, it clamored for "name" players. Ernie Nevers was one of the first stars to capture America's attention. He was a handsome runner from Stanford whom legendary coach Pop Warner claimed was a better player than Jim Thorpe. Nevers began his NFL career with the Duluth (Minnesota) Eskimos, who showcased him on a nationwide tour in 1926, playing 28 of 29 games on the road. He enjoyed his greatest success with the Chicago Cardinals, highlighted by a Thanksgiving Day performance in 1929 when he scored an NFL-record 40 points in a victory over the Bears.

Born: *6/11/03*
Hometown: *Willow River, MN*
College: *Stanford*
NFL Draft: *Free Agent*

Nevers Trivia: *In Ernie's brief baseball career as a pitcher for the St. Louis Browns, he gave up two home runs to what slugger in 1927?*

45

JOE PERRY

Ht: 6'0" Wt: 200 Pro Career: 1948–1963

The San Francisco 49ers discovered Joe Perry while he was playing football at the Alameda Naval Air Station. His ability to burst through holes and avoid defenders earned him the moniker "The Jet." Playing alongside Hugh McElhenny, another Pro Football Hall of Fame running back, he helped make the 49ers' offense one of the NFL's most powerful in the 1950s. Perry rushed for a league-record 8,378 yards and scored 61 touchdowns during his NFL career. He was the first NFL player to run for more than 1,000 yards in consecutive seasons, gaining 1,018 in 1953 and 1,049 in 1954.

Born: 1/27/27
Hometown: Stevens, AR
College: Compton CC (CA)
NFL Draft: Free Agent

Perry Trivia: *Which one of his San Francisco 49ers teammates nicknamed Joe, a high-school track star, "The Jet"?*

Answer: Quarterback Frankie Albert

RICKY WATTERS

Ht: 6'1" Wt: 217 Pro Career: 1991–2001

The biggest moment in Ricky Watters' career came in Super Bowl XXIX, when he tied a Super Bowl record by scoring 3 touchdowns in the 49ers' 49–26 victory. A year earlier, Watters set an NFL postseason record by scoring 5 touchdowns against the New York Giants in a playoff game. The five-time Pro Bowl selection didn't excel just in the postseason. He gained more than 1,000 rushing yards seven times, including a career-high 1,411 in 1996. Despite missing his rookie season with a foot injury, he recovered to rush for 10,643 yards, post 467 receptions, and score 91 touchdowns.

Born: 4/7/69
Hometown: Harrisburg, PA
College: Notre Dame
NFL Draft: 2nd Round, 1991

Watters Trivia: *After four seasons with the 49ers and three seasons with the Eagles, with which NFL team did Ricky end his career?*

ROAD GRADERS

JEROME BETTIS

Ht: 5'11" Wt: 243 Pro Career: 1993-present

Jerome Bettis has been battering defenses since 1993, when the Los Angeles Rams made him the tenth choice in the draft. He began his career with a bang, rushing for 1,429 yards and earning NFL rookie-of-the-year honors. Pittsburgh acquired Bettis in a draft-day trade in 1996, and the power runner fit right in with the blue-collar work ethic of the Steel city. He rushed for more than 1,000 yards six consecutive seasons (1996–2001) and ranks second on the Steelers' career rushing list. The five-time Pro Bowl selection entered 2003 ranked tenth on the NFL's all-time rushing list with 11,542 yards.

Born: 2/16/72
Hometown: Detroit, MI
College: Notre Dame
NFL Draft: 1st Round, 1993

Bettis Trivia: In 2001, Jerome was named the NFL Man of the Year for his contributions in the community. After whom is the award named?

EARL CAMPBELL

Ht: 5'11" Wt: 232 Pro Career: 1978–1985

Few running backs dominated pro football as Earl Campbell did. He was gifted with nifty feet, tremendous speed for his size, and powerful thighs, enabling him to run over or around would-be tacklers. Defenders made higlight films bouching off Campbell, who rushed for 9,407 yards during his Pro Football Hall of Fame career with the Oilers and Saints. He led the NFL each of his first three seasons, including a career-high 1,934 yards in 1980, when he set a record by rushing for more than 200 yards in four games. His 199-yard game against Miami as a rookie in 1978 was one of the best efforts on *NFL Monday Night Football*.

Born: 3/29/55
Hometown: Tyler, TX
College: Texas
NFL Draft: 1st Round, 1978

Campbell Trivia: *What nickname did Campbell earn while winning the Heisman Trophy at the University of Texas in 1977?*

LARRY CSONKA

Ht: 6'3" Wt: 237 Pro Career: 1968–1979

The crowning moment of Larry Csonka's career came in Super Bowl VIII, when he earned MVP honors after rumbling over the Minnesota Vikings for 145 yards and 2 touchdowns. Behind Csonka, the Dolphins posted an easy 24–7 victory. He made his mark with punishing runs between the tackles, and his inside presence opened the outside for teammate Eugene (Mercury) Morris. In 1972, Csonka and Morris became the first teammates to rush for more than 1,000 yards each in the same season. Larry gained 8,081 yards in 11 NFL seasons, and helped Miami win two NFL titles.

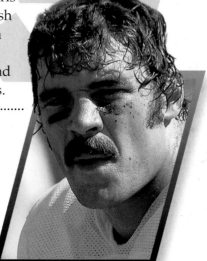

Born: 12/25/46
Hometown: Stow, OH
College: Syracuse
NFL Draft: 1st Round, 1968

Csonka Trivia: Larry rushed for 112 yards to help Miami defeat Washington 14–7 in Super Bowl VII. What was the Dolphins' final record that year?

JOHN HENRY JOHNSON

Ht: *6'2"* **Wt:** *210* **Pro Career:** *1954–1966*

John Henry Johnson was known for his durability and power. The bruising fullback played 13 seasons for four different teams (San Francisco, 1954–56; Detroit, 1957–59; Pittsburgh, 1960–65; and Houston, 1966). Johnson's greatest seasons statistically were with Pittsburgh in 1962 (a career-high 1,141 rushing yards and 9 touchdowns to equal his personal best) and 1964 (1,048 yards). In 1957, he helped propel the Detroit Lions to the NFL championship. Johnson finished his career in the AFL with the Oilers and was fourth on pro football's all-time rushing list (6,803 yards) when he retired.

Born: *11/24/29*
Hometown: *Waterproof, LA*
College: *Arizona State*
NFL Draft: *2nd Round, 1953*

Johnson Trivia: *During John Henry's first three NFL seasons, the 49ers' running backs and quarterbacks were known by what nickname?*

MARION MOTLEY

Ht: *6'1"* **Wt:** *232* **Pro Career:** *1946–1955*

Marion Motley was such a gifted player that his coach with the Cleveland Browns, the legendary Paul Brown, said that if he had played solely on defense, he could have been one of the game's greatest linebackers. Instead, he was one of the greatest running backs. Motley joined the Browns of the AAFC in 1946, and went with them when they joined the NFL. In 1950, he was the league's leading rusher. His most remarkable game came against Pittsburgh in 1950, when he gained 188 yards in 11 carries—a record-setting 17.1 yards per attempt. He averaged 5.7 yards per carry during his pro career.

Born: *6/5/20*
Hometown: *Leesburg, GA*
College: *Nevada-Reno*
NFL Draft: *Free Agent*

Motley Trivia: *After retiring and sitting out the 1954 season, Marion briefly tried a comeback with what team?*

60

BRONKO NAGURSKI

Ht: *6'2"* **Wt:** *226* **Pro Career:** *1930–37, 1943*

Bronko Nagurski played when there were no facemasks and players wore leather helmets, but that didn't deter him from flying headlong into every play. He was an All-America player at both fullback and tackle while at the University of Minnesota. In the NFL, he spent time at tackle and linebacker when he wasn't at running back for the Chicago Bears. His scoring pass was the lone touchdown in the 1932 playoff game. In 1943, he came out of retirement to help the Bears win the NFL title. He was a charter member of the Pro Football Hall of Fame.

Born: *11/3/08*
Hometown: *Rainy River, Canada*
College: *Minnesota*
NFL Draft: *Free Agent*

Nagurski Trivia: *Bronko also earned national prominence as a professional wrestler. What was this tough guy's real name?*

Answer: Bronislau

JOHN RIGGINS

Ht: 6'2" Wt: 230 Pro Career: 1971–1985

There was nothing mysterious about John Riggins' running style, which relied on brute strength, fierce competitiveness, and surprising speed. Nicknamed "The Diesel" for all the defenders he flattened, he totaled 11,352 rushing yards and 116 touchdowns for the New York Jets and Washington Redskins. His most impressive efforts came during the 1982 playoffs when he rushed 136 times for 610 yards in four games. His MVP performance in the Redskins' Super Bowl XVII victory—166 rushing yards, including a 43-yard touchdown run that gave the Redskins the lead in the fourth quarter—served as the exclamation point.

Born: 8/4/49
Hometown: Centralia, KS
College: Kansas
NFL Draft: 1st Round, 1971

Riggins Trivia: *What was the famous nickname of the offensive line that blocked for John during his seasons with the Redskins?*

JIM TAYLOR

Ht: *6'0"* **Wt:** *214* **Pro Career:** *1958–1967*

Jim Brown was the most prominent running back during the 1960s, but Jim Taylor ran a close second. A bruising fullback, Taylor was perfectly suited for Vince Lombardi's power rushing attack in Green Bay. In 1962, Taylor gained a personal-best 1,474 yards to interrupt Brown's five-year hold on the rushing title. Strength, toughness, and determination helped Taylor overcome what he lacked in athletic ability. He finished his NFL career second to Brown on the all-time rushing list with 8,597 yards. Taylor helped the Packers win four NFL championships and Super Bowl I.

Born: *9/20/35*
Hometown: *Baton Rouge, LA*
College: *Louisiana State*
NFL Draft: *2nd Round, 1958*

Taylor Trivia: *Jim played 9 of his 10 NFL seasons with the Green Bay Packers. With which team did he play his final season?*

STEVE VAN BUREN

Ht: 6'0" Wt: 200 Pro Career: 1944–1951

Steve Van Buren was a punishing runner and blocker who led the NFL in rushing four times and retired as the league's all-time leading rusher with 5,860 yards. He twice led the Philadelphia Eagles to NFL titles. He ran for 98 yards and scored the game's only touchdown in the Eagles' 7–0 victory over the Cardinals in the 1948 title game, and set a championship game record with 196 rushing yards in a victory over the Rams in 1949. But Van Buren was more than a power runner. Deceptively fast, he twice led the league in kickoff returns, and returned 5 of his 110 career kickoff and punt returns for touchdowns.

Born: 12/28/20
Hometown: La Ceiba, Honduras
College: Louisiana State
NFL Draft: 1st Round, 1944

Van Buren Trivia: *Steve retired as the league's all-time leader in rushing touchdowns after eight seasons with the Eagles. How many did he score?*

SHOWSTOPPERS

OTTIS ANDERSON

Ht: 6'2" Wt: 220 Pro Career: 1979–1992

Ottis Anderson burst on to the NFL scene by rushing for 191 yards in his first game. He went on to set an NFL rookie record for most rushing attempts in a season (331), which proved to be the start of a brilliant career. During his years with the St. Louis Cardinals (1979–1986), Anderson was known for his quick-cutting ability and speed. He rushed for more than 1,000 yards in five of his first six seasons. The New York Giants acquired Anderson four games into the 1986 season, and it proved to be a wise move. The two-time Pro Bowl selection evolved into more of a power runner and helped the Giants win Super Bowl XXV.

Born: 1/19/57
Hometown: W. Palm Beach, FL
College: Miami
NFL Draft: 1st Round, 1979

Anderson Trivia: *Ottis was named the MVP of Super Bowl XXV after rushing for 102 yards and a touchdown. Whom did the Giants defeat?*

CHARLIE GARNER

Ht: *5'9"* **Wt:** *187* **Pro Career:** *1994–present*

No matter which team Charlie Garner has played for during his NFL career (Philadelphia, 1994–98; San Francisco, 1999–2000; and Oakland, 2001–present), he has generated offensive excitement. In 1995, the speedy runner, who excels at changing directions, led the league by averaging 5.4 yards per carry. In each of his two seasons with the 49ers, he rushed for more than 1,000 yards and caught more than 50 passes. Arguably, his best season was 2002, when he helped the Raiders earn a Super Bowl berth by rushing for 962 yards (5.3 yards per carry) and catching 91 passes for 941 yards.

Born: **2/13/72**
Hometown: **Falls Church, VA**
College: **Tennessee**
NFL Draft: **2nd Round, 1994**

Garner Trivia: *Against which team did Charlie set Raiders' playoff records for rushing yards in a game (158) and longest run (80 yards)?*

RED GRANGE

Ht: 6'0" Wt: 180 Pro Career: 1925–1934

Known as the "Galloping Ghost" at the University of Illinois because of his elusive running style, Harold (Red) Grange was one of the most exciting players of his day. His marquee value played a pivotal role in establishing the fledgling NFL as a legitimate sports league. In 1925, he played five games with the Chicago Bears before he and the Bears embarked on a coast-to-coast barnstorming tour. With Grange as the drawing card, the Bears played in front of more than 400,000 fans during the next two months. As a runner and defensive back, Grange helped the Bears win two NFL titles.

Born: *6/13/03*
Hometown: *Forksville, PA*
College: *Illinois*
NFL Draft: *Free Agent*

Grange Trivia: A national star, Red signed a Hollywood movie contract during his barnstorming tour. What was the first movie in which he starred?

PAUL HORNUNG

Ht: 6'2" Wt: 215 Pro Career: 1957–1966

Despite playing for a team with a losing record, Paul Hornung won the Heisman Trophy as a quarterback at Notre Dame. He switched to running back after he joined the Green Bay Packers and went on to earn a spot in the Pro Football Hall of Fame. Hornung was a multi-dimensional offensive threat who could run, pass, and kick. His greatest season came in 1960, when he was the league's MVP after scoring an NFL-record 176 points (15 touchdowns, 15 field goals, 41 extra points). Nicknamed "The Golden Boy" for his Hollywood looks, he helped the Packers win four NFL championships.

Born: 12/23/35
Hometown: Louisville, KY
College: Notre Dame
NFL Draft: 1st Round, 1957

Hornung Trivia: *What Pro Football Hall of Fame player was Hornung's backfield running mate during most of his career?*

BO JACKSON

Ht: 6'1" Wt: 227 Pro Career: 1987–1990

Bo Jackson played only four seasons, but he provided a career's worth of highlights during his short tenure. After he won the 1985 Heisman Trophy at Auburn, Tampa Bay made him the first overall choice in the 1986 NFL Draft. Jackson, though, had other ideas, and he signed with major league baseball's Kansas City Royals rather than play in the NFL. The Raiders selected Jackson when he again was eligible for the draft the following year, and they were willing to wait until after baseball season. The dynamic runner proved to be a threat every time he touched the ball, scoring 18 touchdowns in 38 games.

Born: 11/30/62
Hometown: Bessemer, AL
College: Auburn
NFL Draft: 7th Round, 1987

Jackson Trivia: *Thanks to an assortment of commercial endorsements, Bo Jackson became a household name. What is Bo's given name?*

OLLIE MATSON

Ht: **6'2"** *Wt:* **220** *Pro Career:* **1952–1966**

Ollie Matson seemed to have a big play in him each time he stepped on a football field. Big and incredibly fast—he won a gold medal in the 1,600-meter relay at the 1952 Summer Olympics—he was a dangerous running back, receiver, defensive back, and kick returner. During a 14-year career, Matson scored 73 total touchdowns (40 rushing, 23 receiving, 9 on kick returns, and 1 on a fumble recovery). He led the NFL in punt-return average in 1955 and kickoff-return average in 1958. He was so valued that in 1959 the Rams traded nine players to acquire him from the Cardinals.

Born: **5/1/30**
Hometown: **Trinity, TX**
College: **San Francisco**
NFL Draft: **1st Round, 1952**

Matson Trivia: *In what individual event did Ollie win a bronze medal at the 1952 Summer Olympic Games in Helsinki, Finland?*

HUGH MCELHENNY

Ht: 6'1" Wt: 195 Pro Career: 1952–1964

Hugh McElhenny announced his arrival in 1952 by averaging 7 yards per carry and scoring 10 times. From the outset, he was poetry in motion, darting, turning, and twisting through defenders. Many of his runs covered more yards than reflected in statistics because he crisscrossed the field, searching for open spaces. He was one of the most feared open-field runners in the game. His best year may have come in 1961, when he compiled 1,067 all-purpose yards for the expansion Vikings. McElhenny was selected to six Pro Bowls, scored 60 touchdowns, and gained 11,369 total yards from scrimmage.

Born: 12/31/28
Hometown: Los Angeles, CA
College: Washington
NFL Draft: 1st Round, 1952

McElhenny Trivia: Hugh was one of the most exciting runners ever. What was the nickname he earned because of his athletic ability?

Answer: The King

LENNY MOORE

Ht: 6'1" Wt: 191 Pro Career: 1956–1967

Lenny Moore helped revolutionize the running back position by displaying equal ability as a runner (he averaged more than 7 yards per carry in three seasons) and receiver (twice he averaged more than 20 yards per catch). During his 12-year NFL career with the Baltimore Colts, he rushed for 5,174 yards and caught passes for another 6,039 yards. He ranked second in NFL history with 113 touchdowns when he retired, highlighted by a stretch in which he scored touchdowns in 18 consecutive games, an NFL record that still stands. In 1964, he became the first player to score 20 touchdowns in a season.

Born: **11/25/33**
Hometown: **Reading, PA**
College: **Penn State**
NFL Draft: **1st Round, 1956**

Moore Trivia: *Lenny's practice of wrapping white tape over the top of his black shoes earned him what nickname?*

GALE SAYERS

Ht: 6'0" Wt: 198 Pro Career: 1965–1971

Though Gale Sayers played only seven NFL seasons because of knee injuries, he was such an electrifying player that he earned a spot in the Pro Football Hall of Fame in 1977, his first year of eligibility. At age 34, he is the youngest player so honored. Nicknamed the Kansas Comet in college, Sayers scored a league-record 22 touchdowns in his rookie season with the Bears. Included among his scores were a kickoff return of 96 yards, a punt return of 85 yards, a 61-yard run, and receptions of 80 yards (twice) and 65 yards. He scored 6 touchdowns against the 49ers to tie the NFL single-game record.

Born: 5/30/43
Hometown: Wichita, KS
College: Kansas
NFL Draft: 1st Round, 1965

Sayers Trivia: *Sayers' unlikely friendship with which Chicago Bears teammate was the basis for the memorable TV movie* Brian's Song?

THURMAN THOMAS

Ht: **5'10"** *Wt:* **198** *Pro Career:* **1988–2000**

Behind Thurman Thomas, the Buffalo Bills became one of the NFL's best teams, playing in four consecutive Super Bowls from 1990–93. Thomas, a second-round draft choice in 1988, was a nifty runner with quick feet. His disappointment at not being a first-round pick served as motivation throughout his 13-year career. Thomas, who entered 2003 ranked ninth on the NFL's all-time list with 12,074 rushing yards, posted eight consecutive 1,000-yard seasons (1989–1996). He had 46 games with 100 or more rushing yards, scored 88 touchdowns, and earned five Pro Bowl selections.

Born: **5/16/66**
Hometown: **Houston, TX**
College: **Oklahoma State**
NFL Draft: **2nd Round, 1988**

Thomas Trivia: *Thurman ranks third on the NFL's all-time postseason rushing list with 1,442 yards. What two running backs are ahead of him?*

JIM THORPE

Ht: 6'1" Wt: 202 Pro Career: 1915–1928

Jim Thorpe was such an incredible physical specimen that in 1950, sportswriters selected him as the greatest athlete of the first half of the 20th century. A Sac and Fox Indian, Thorpe was an outstanding baseball player and track star, but it was on the football field where he first gained fame as an All-America college player. He starred in the pre-NFL days for the Canton Bulldogs, leading them to three championships. He served as the league's president in 1920. In the 1912 Olympics, Thorpe won gold medals in the pentathlon and decathlon.

Born: 5/28/1887
Hometown: Prague, OK
College: Carlisle
NFL Draft: Free Agent

Thorpe Trivia: *Jim also played major league baseball. He was a good fielder but not a very good hitter. With which team did he play the majority of his six-year career?*

THE NEXT GENERATION

SHAUN ALEXANDER

Ht: 5'11" Wt: 220 Pro Career: 2000–present

Shaun Alexander was an All-America running back in both high school and college, where he was Alabama's all-time leading rusher. Nothing has changed for Alexander, as he has been an offensive force for the Seahawks since taking over the starting role in 2001. He gained 1,318 rushing yards and led the NFL with 14 rushing touchdowns that season. The highlight was a club-record 266-yard, 3-touchdown effort, in a 34–27 victory over the Oakland Raiders. In 2002, he rushed for 1,175 yards, and led the NFC in total touchdowns (18) and rushing touchdowns (16). Both marks are club records.

Born: 8/30/77
Hometown: Florence, KY
College: Alabama
NFL Draft: 1st Round, 2000

Alexander Trivia: *Shaun is only the third running back drafted by the Seahawks in the first round. Who were the others?*

Answer: Curt Warner, 1983; John L. Williams, 1986

AHMAN GREEN

Ht: 6'0" Wt: 213 Pro Career: 1998–present

The passing exploits of Brett Favre usually dominate the headlines in Green Bay, but during the 2000–02 seasons, Ahman Green shared the spotlight with the three-time NFL MVP. The added balance Green supplied to the Packers' offense helped them stay among the league's elite teams. Green, a runner with amazing quickness, wastes few moves. He is only the third running back in Green Bay history to rush for more than 1,000 yards in three consecutive seasons. The two-time Pro Bowl choice also caught 50 or more passes each year since joining the Packers.

Born: 2/16/77
Hometown: Omaha, NE
College: Nebraska
NFL Draft: 3rd Round, 1998

Green Trivia: *Ahman, whose 1,387 rushing yards in 2001 are the third most in Packers' history, was acquired by Green Bay in a trade with which team?*

TRAVIS HENRY

Ht: 5'9" Wt: 220 Pro Career: 2001–present

It's never easy to replace a legend, but just three years after Thurman Thomas left Buffalo, the Bills have found another gem. Travis Henry, the all-time leading rusher at Tennessee, used his quickness and cutting ability to rush for 1,438 yards and 13 touchdowns in 2002, his second NFL season. He ranked fifth in the NFL in yards, his rushing touchdown total was the highest for a Bills' player since 1975, and he played in his first Pro Bowl following the season. Henry also rushed for at least 100 yards in six games—the most 100-yard games since Thomas had seven in 1993.

Born: 10/29/78
Hometown: Frostproof, FL
College: Tennessee
NFL Draft: 2nd Round, 2001

Henry Trivia: *Travis rushed for 159 yards against Houston in 2002—the best performance in club history since what Bills runner gained 181 in 1992?*

PRIEST HOLMES

Ht: 5'9" Wt: 205 Pro Career: 1997–present

When head coach Dick Vermeil led the Rams to victory in Super Bowl XXXIV, he made good use of running back Marshall Faulk. When Vermeil became the Chiefs' head coach in 2001, he found another multitalented running back in Priest Holmes, a free agent from the Ravens who had been underutilized in Baltimore. Holmes excelled in his new role with the Chiefs, rushing for 1,555 yards and catching 62 passes in 2001. In 2002, he earned his second Pro Bowl selection and led the NFL with 24 touchdowns and 2,287 total yards from scrimmage (1,615 rushing and 672 receiving).

Born: 10/7/73
Hometown: Fort Smith, AR
College: Texas
NFL Draft: Free Agent

Holmes Trivia: *Priest set Chiefs season records for rushing yards and touchdowns. Who held the previous records in each category, respectively?*

EDGERRIN JAMES

Ht: 6'0" Wt: 214 Pro Career: 1999–present

As a junior at the University of Miami, Edgerrin James broke Ottis Anderson's school records for rushing yards (1,416) and touchdowns (17) in a season. James has continued smashing records as a member of the Colts, earning NFL offensive rookie of the year honors and winning the NFL rushing title in each of his first two seasons. An extremely versatile back, he was the first player in NFL history to post consecutive seasons with more than 1,500 rushing yards and 500 receiving yards. James set a franchise record with 1,709 rushing yards in 2000. He also led the AFC in touchdowns in 1999 and 2000.

Born: 8/1/78
Hometown: Immokalee, FL
College: Miami
NFL Draft: 1st Round, 1999

James Trivia: *Through the first 26 games of his NFL career, Edgerrin scored 31 touchdowns. Who is the only other NFL player to equal that feat?*

JAMAL LEWIS

Ht: 5'11" Wt: 231 Pro Career: 2000–present

Jamal Lewis, the fifth player selected in the 2000 NFL Draft, was one of the final pieces to the puzzle that helped the Baltimore Ravens to their first Super Bowl title. As the youngest offensive player in the league his rookie season, the powerful Lewis anchored a ball-control offense and set a club record with 1,364 rushing yards in the Ravens' 12–4 season. He had 102 yards and scored a touchdown in a 34–7 victory over the New York Giants in Super Bowl XXXV. Lewis, who missed the 2001 season because of a knee injury, rebounded in 2002 to finish eighth in the NFL with 1,327 rushing yards.

Born: 8/28/79
Hometown: Atlanta, GA
College: Tennessee
NFL Draft: 1st Round, 2000

Lewis Trivia: *Who is the only NFL running back besides Jamal to rush for more than 1,000 yards and win a Super Bowl ring as a rookie?*

Answer: Tony Dorsett

DEUCE McALLISTER

Ht: *6'1"* **Wt:** *222* **Pro Career:** *2001–present*

The New Orleans Saints knew what they were doing when they traded Ricky Williams to the Miami Dolphins before the 2002 season and inserted Deuce McAllister, the club's top draft pick in 2001, into the starting lineup. The quicker and more versatile McAllister was a better fit for New Orleans' offensive scheme. McAllister, the all-time leading rusher at Mississippi, led the NFC with 1,388 rushing yards in 2002 and scored 16 touchdowns (both marks rank second in club history). He also had 47 catches, (second most on the team) en route to his first Pro Bowl appearance.

Born: *12/27/78*
Hometown: *Morton, MS*
College: *Mississippi*
NFL Draft: *1st Round, 2001*

McAllister Trivia: *Deuce is a nickname given to McAllister by his high school coach. What is Deuce's given name?*

CLINTON PORTIS

Ht: 5'11" Wt: 204 Pro Career: 2002-present

The Denver Broncos already had three 1,000-yard rushers on their roster (Terrell Davis, Mike Anderson, and Olandis Gary) when they made Clinton Portis a second-round draft choice in 2002. As it turned out, they were adding a fourth. Portis, the NFL offensive rookie of the year, started 12 games, averaging a franchise-record 5.52 yards per carry and rushing for a club rookie record 1,508 yards and 15 touchdowns. He also had 33 receptions for 364 yards. He finished the season by rushing for more than 100 yards in four of the last five games, including a 228-yard effort and a 4-touchdown game.

Born: 9/1/81
Hometown: Gainesville, FL
College: Miami
NFL Draft: 2nd Round, 2002

Portis Trivia: *Clinton wears jersey number 26. What other 1,000-yard Broncos running back wore the same number?*

LaDainian Tomlinson

Ht: 5'10" Wt: 221 Pro Career: 2001–present

When the Chargers traded the first overall choice in the 2001 NFL Draft (Michael Vick) to Atlanta, they held their breath and hoped the player they wanted, LaDainian Tomlinson, would still be available four picks later. The All-America running back, who had rushed for 2,158 yards his senior season, was still available and drafted by the Chargers. He gained 1,236 yards as a rookie—the second highest total in franchise history—and was even better in 2002. Tomlinson set club records for carries (372) and rushing yards (1,683), caught 79 passes, scored 15 touchdowns, and earned his first trip to the Pro Bowl.

Born: 6/23/79
Hometown: Rosebud, TX
College: Texas Christian
NFL Draft: 1st Round, 2001

Tomlinson Trivia: *LaDainian set the Chargers' record for total yards from scrimmage in his rookie season. Whose record did he break?*

RICKY WILLIAMS

Ht: 5'10" Wt: 230 Pro Career: 1999–present

After setting 20 NCAA records, including most career rushing yards, Ricky Williams won the Heisman Trophy as the nation's best college player in 1998. The New Orleans Saints were so impressed that they traded all six of their choices in the 1999 NFL Draft and two selections in 2000 to acquire him. Blessed with the combination of power and speed, Williams rushed for 3,129 yards in his first three seasons with the Saints before being traded to Miami in 2002. He also made an immediate impact with the Dolphins, leading the NFL with 1,853 rushing yards, and becoming just the third player to post consecutive 200-yard rushing games.

Born: 5/21/77
Hometown: San Diego, CA
College: Texas
NFL Draft: 1st Round, 1999

Williams Trivia: *Ricky set a Dolphins' record with 1,853 rushing yards in 2002. Who held the old record?*

Answer: Delvin Williams

STATISTICS

SHAUN ALEXANDER (for more information, see pages 96–97)

| YR. | TEAM | G | RUSHING | | | | RECEIVING | | | | TOTAL |
			ATT	YDS	AVG	TD	REC	YDS	AVG	TD	TD
2000	Seattle	16	64	313	4.9	2	5	41	8.2	0	2
2001	Seattle	16	309	1,318	4.3	14*	44	343	7.8	2	16
2002	Seattle	16	295	1,175	4.0	16	59	460	7.8	2	18
Totals		**48**	**668**	**2,806**	**4.2**	**32**	**108**	**844**	**7.8**	**4**	**36**

*Led league

Transactions
• Selected by Seattle Seahawks in first round (19th pick overall) of the 2000 NFL Draft.

Noteworthy
• Became first NFL player to score 5 touchdowns in a half (first half vs. Minnesota, Sept. 29, 2002);
• Set Seahawks records with 18 total touchdowns and 16 rushing touchdowns in 2002;
• In his two seasons as a starter, has finished tied for second (2001) and second (2002) in the NFL in touchdowns;
• Rushed for a career-high 266 yards against Oakland (Nov. 11, 2001);
• Longest run from scrimmage was 88 yards against Oakland (Nov. 11, 2001);
• Longest reception was 80 yards against Minnesota (Sept. 29, 2002);
• The fourth running back selected in the 2000 draft; after three seasons Alexander has scored almost as many touchdowns (36) as the other three running back selections combined (Jamal Lewis, Thomas Jones, and Ron Dayne combined for 37 touchdowns from 2000–02);
• All-time leading rusher at the University of Alabama;
• Earned bachelor's degree in marketing at Alabama in 1999;
• All-America high school running back as chosen by *Parade* magazine and *USA Today*;
• Kentucky high school player of the year at Boone County High.

MARCUS ALLEN (for more information, see pages 8–9)

| YR. | TEAM | G | RUSHING | | | | RECEIVING | | | | TOTAL |
			ATT	YDS	AVG	TD	REC	YDS	AVG	TD	TD
1982	L.A. Raiders	9	160	697	4.4	11*	38	401	10.6	3	14*
1983	L.A. Raiders	16	266	1,014	3.8	9	68	590	8.7	2	12
1984	L.A. Raiders	16	275	1.168	4.2	13	64	758	11.8	5	18*
1985	L.A. Raiders	16	380	1,759*	4.6	11	67	555	8.3	3	14
1986	L.A. Raiders	13	208	759	3.6	5	46	453	9.8	2	7
1987	L.A. Raiders	12	200	754	3.8	5	51	410	8.0	0	5
1988	L.A. Raiders	15	223	831	3.7	7	34	303	8.9	1	8
1989	L.A. Raiders	8	69	293	4.2	2	20	191	9.6	0	2
1990	L.A. Raiders	16	179	682	3.8	12	15	189	12.6	1	13
1991	L.A. Raiders	8	63	287	4.6	2	15	131	8.7	0	2
1992	L.A. Raiders	16	67	301	4.5	2	28	277	9.9	1	3
1993	Kansas City	16	206	764	3.7	12*	34	238	7.0	3	15
1994	Kansas City	13	189	709	3.8	7	42	349	8.3	0	7
1995	Kansas City	16	207	890	4.3	5	27	210	7.8	0	5
1996	Kansas City	16	206	830	4.0	9	27	270	10.0	0	9
1997	Kansas City	16	124	505	4.1	11	11	86	7.8	0	11
Totals		**222**	**3,022**	**12,243**	**4.1**	**123**	**587**	**5,411**	**9.2**	**21**	**145**

*Led league

Transactions
- Selected by L.A. Raiders in first round (10th pick overall) of the 1982 NFL Draft;
- Granted unconditional free agency, signed with Kansas City Chiefs (June 9, 1993).

Noteworthy
- Inducted into the Pro Football Hall of Fame in 2003;
- 1985 NFL most valuable player;
- 1982 NFL rookie of the year;
- Selected to six Pro Bowls (following the 1982, 1984–87, and 1993 seasons);
- Set Super Bowl record with a 74-yard touchdown run in the Raiders' 38–9 victory over the Redskins in Super Bowl XVIII and was named the game's most valuable player after rushing for 191 yards and 2 scores;
- Retired as the NFL's all-time leader with 145 rushing touchdowns. Cowboys running back Emmitt Smith has since surpassed Allen;
- Won the Heisman Trophy, Walter Camp Award, and Maxwell Award as the nation's best college player after rushing for a then-NCAA record 2,342 yards during senior season at the University of Southern California in 1981;
- Set 12 NCAA records at USC, including most 200-yard rushing games (11);
- All-America quarterback and defensive back at Lincoln High School in San Diego;
- Brother Damon Allen is the all-time leading passer in Canadian Football League history.

OTTIS ANDERSON (for more information, see pages 72–73)

			RUSHING				RECEIVING				TOTAL
YR.	TEAM	G	ATT	YDS	AVG	TD	REC	YDS	AVG	TD	TD
1979	St. Louis	16	331	1,605	4.8	8	41	308	7.5	2	10
1980	St. Louis	16	301	1,352	4.5	9	36	308	8.6	0	9
1981	St. Louis	16	328	1,376	4.2	9	51	387	7.6	0	9
1982	St. Louis	8	145	587	4.0	3	14	106	7.6	0	3
1983	St. Louis	15	296	1,270	4.3	5	54	459	8.5	1	6
1984	St. Louis	15	289	1,174	4.1	6	70	611	8.7	2	8
1985	St. Louis	9	117	479	4.1	4	23	225	9.8	0	4
1986	St. Louis	4	51	156	3.1	2	10	91	9.1	0	2
1986	N.Y. Giants	8	24	81	3.4	1	9	46	5.1	0	1
1987	N.Y. Giants	4	2	6	3.0	0	2	16	8.0	0	0
1988	N.Y. Giants	16	65	208	3.2	8	9	57	6.3	0	8
1989	N.Y. Giants	16	325	1,023	3.1	14	28	268	9.6	0	14
1990	N.Y. Giants	16	225	784	3.5	11	18	139	7.7	0	11
1991	N.Y. Giants	10	53	141	2.7	1	11	41	3.7	0	1
1992	N.Y. Giants	13	10	31	3.1	0	0	0	—	0	0
Totals		182	2,562	10,273	4.0	81	376	3,062	8.1	5	86

Transactions
- Selected by St. Louis Cardinals in first round (eighth pick overall) of the 1979 NFL Draft;
- Traded by Cardinals to New York Giants for second- (traded) and seventh-round (TE William Harris) choices in the 1987 draft (Oct. 8, 1986).

Noteworthy
- Selected to two Pro Bowls (following the 1979 and 1980 seasons);
- 1979 NFL rookie of the year;
- 1989 NFL comeback player of the year;
- Named most valuable player of Super Bowl XXV after rushing for 102 yards and a touchdown in the Giants' 20–19 victory over the Buffalo Bills;
- Scored one touchdown in the Giants' 39–20 victory over Denver in Super Bowl XXI;
- Finished his NFL career in eighth place on the league's all-time rushing list;
- Trails only Eric Dickerson (1,808 yards in 1983) and George Rogers (1,674 in 1981) for most rushing yards in a rookie season in NFL history;
- Rushed for a career-high 193 yards against Dallas in NFL debut (Sept. 2, 1979);
- Longest run from scrimmage was a 76-yard touchdown against Dallas (Sept. 2, 1979);
- Longest reception was 57 yards against the Giants (Nov. 18, 1984);
- All-America at the University of Miami and was first Hurricanes running back to rush for more than 1,000 yards in a season (1,266 in 1978).

TIKI BARBER (for more information, see pages 28–29)

| YR. | TEAM | G | RUSHING | | | | RECEIVING | | | | TOTAL |
			ATT	YDS	AVG	TD	REC	YDS	AVG	TD	TD
1997	N.Y. Giants	12	136	511	3.8	3	34	299	8.8	1	4
1998	N.Y. Giants	16	52	166	3.2	0	42	348	8.3	3	3
1999	N.Y. Giants	16	62	258	4.2	0	66	609	9.2	2	3
2000	N.Y. Giants	16	213	1,006	4.7	8	70	719	10.3	1	9
2001	N.Y. Giants	14	166	865	5.2	4	72	577	8.0	0	4
2002	N.Y. Giants	16	304	1,387	4.6	11	68	587	8.7	0	11
Totals		**90**	**933**	**4,193**	**4.5**	**26**	**352**	**3,149**	**9.0**	**7**	**34**

Transactions
• Selected by N.Y. Giants in second round (36th pick overall) of the 1997 NFL Draft.

Noteworthy
• Returned 27 kickoffs for 544 yards for career;
• Returned 122 punts for 1,181 yards and a touchdown for career;
• Rushing yards in 2002 were second most in a season in Giants history;
• Gained career-high 203 yards (second-highest single-game total in club history) against Philadelphia (Dec. 28, 2002);
• Longest run from scrimmage was 78-yard touchdown against Arizona (Sept. 3, 2000);
• Longest reception was an 87-yard touchdown catch against Arizona (Dec. 6, 1998);
• All-time leading rusher (3,389) at the University of Virginia;
• Competed with identical twin brother Ronde for Virginia's track team;
• Super Prep High School All-America running back at Cave Spring High in Roanoke, Virginia;
• Won Virginia high school long jump and triple jump titles as a senior;
• Full name is Atiim Kiambu Barber.

JEROME BETTIS (for more information, see pages 52–53)

| YR. | TEAM | G | RUSHING | | | | RECEIVING | | | | TOTAL |
			ATT	YDS	AVG	TD	REC	YDS	AVG	TD	TD
1993	L.A. Rams	16	294	1,429	4.9	7	26	244	9.4	0	7
1994	L.A. Rams	16	319	1,025	3.2	3	31	293	9.5	1	4
1995	St. Louis	15	183	637	3.5	3	18	106	5.9	0	3
1996	Pittsburgh	16	320	1,431	4.5	11	22	122	5.5	0	11
1997	Pittsburgh	15	375*	1,665	4.4	7	15	110	7.3	2	9
1998	Pittsburgh	15	316	1,185	3.8	3	16	90	5.6	0	3
1999	Pittsburgh	16	299	1,091	3.6	7	21	110	5.2	0	7
2000	Pittsburgh	16	355	1,341	3.8	8	13	97	7.5	0	8
2001	Pittsburgh	11	225	1,072	4.8	4	8	48	6.0	0	4
2002	Pittsburgh	13	187	666	3.6	9	7	57	8.1	0	9
Totals		**149**	**2,894**	**11,542**	**4.0**	**63**	**178**	**1,277**	**7.2**	**3**	**66**

*Led league

Transactions
- Selected by the L.A. Rams in first round (10th pick overall) of 1993 NFL Draft;
- Traded by Rams with third-round draft pick (LB Steven Conley) in 1996 draft to Steelers for second-round pick (TE Ernie Conwell) in 1996 NFL Draft and fourth-round pick (traded) in 1997 NFL Draft (April 20, 1996).

Noteworthy
- Selected to four Pro Bowls (following the 1993, 1994, 1996, and 1997 seasons);
- Named 1993 NFL rookie of the year;
- Named 2001 NFL/Walter Payton Man of the Year;
- Twelfth running back in NFL history to surpass 11,000 career rushing yards;
- Second on the Steelers' all-time rushing list with 8,541 yards;
- Played in 1997 and 2001 AFC Championship Games;
- Has rushed for 329 yards and 4 touchdowns and caught 7 passes for 36 yards in postseason during NFL career;
- Rushed for a career-high 212 yards against New Orleans (Dec. 12, 1993);
- Longest run was for a 71-yard touchdown against New Orleans (Dec. 12, 1993);
- Longest reception was 34 yards against the Giants (Oct. 16, 1994);
- Completed 2 of 5 career pass attempts for 53 yards, 2 touchdowns, and 1 interception;
- Nicknamed "The Bus";
- Averaged 5.7 yards per carry during college career at Notre Dame;
- Played on same high school team (McKenzie High in Detroit) as Packers defensive tackle Gilbert Brown.

JIM BROWN

(for more information, see pages 10–11)

| Yr. | Team | G | RUSHING | | | | RECEIVING | | | | Total |
			Att	Yds	Avg	TD	Rec	Yds	Avg	TD	TD
1957	Cleveland	12	202	942*	4.7	9*	16	55	3.4	1	10
1958	Cleveland	12	257*	1,527*	5.9	17*	16	138	8.6	1	18*
1959	Cleveland	12	290*	1,329*	4.6	14*	24	190	7.9	0	14*
1960	Cleveland	12	215	1,257*	5.8	9	19	204	10.7	2	11
1961	Cleveland	14	305*	1,408*	4.6	8	46	459	10.0	2	10
1962	Cleveland	14	230	996	4.3	13	47	517	11.0	5	18
1963	Cleveland	14	291*	1,863*	6.4*	12*	24	268	11.2	3	15*
1964	Cleveland	14	280*	1,446*	5.2*	7	36	340	9.4	2	9
1965	Cleveland	14	289*	1,544*	5.3	17*	34	328	9.6	4	21
Totals		**118**	**2,359**	**12,312**	**5.2***	**106**	**262**	**2,499**	**9.5**	**20**	**126**

*Led league

Transactions
• Selected by Cleveland Browns in first round (sixth overall pick) of the 1957 NFL Draft.

Noteworthy
• Inducted into the Pro Football Hall of Fame in 1971;
• 1957 and 1965 NFL most valuable player;
• 1957 NFL rookie of the year;
• Selected to the Pro Bowl in each of his nine NFL seasons;
• Rushed for 114 yards to lead the Browns to a 27–0 victory over Baltimore in the 1964 NFL Championship Game;
• Finished his NFL career as the league's all-time leading rusher. Brown's record lasted until it was surpassed by Walter Payton in 1984;
• Holds NFL all-time records for most seasons leading the league in rushing (8), most seasons leading the league in rushing attempts (6), average yards per carry (5.2) by a running back, and most seasons leading the league in rushing touchdowns (5);
• Finished his NFL career as the league's all-time leader in rushing and total touchdowns, most 100-yard games (58), most 1,000-yard seasons, and most 200-yard games (4);
• Set an NFL rookie record with 237 rushing yards against the Rams (Nov. 24, 1957);
• His uniform number 32 is retired by the Browns;
• All-America running back at Syracuse University;
• All-America lacrosse player and letterman in basketball at Syracuse.

EARL CAMPBELL (for more information, see pages 54–55)

| YR. | TEAM | G | RUSHING | | | | RECEIVING | | | | TOTAL |
			ATT	YDS	AVG	TD	REC	YDS	AVG	TD	TD
1978	Houston	15	302	1,450*	4.8	13	12	48	4.0	0	13
1979	Houston	16	368	1,697*	4.6	19*	16	94	5.9	0	19*
1980	Houston	15	373*	1,934*	5.2*	13*	11	47	4.3	0	13
1981	Houston	16	361	1,376	3.8	10	36	156	4.3	0	10
1982	Houston	9	157	538	3.4	2	18	130	7.2	0	2
1983	Houston	14	322	1,301	4.0	12	19	216	11.4	0	12
1984	Houston	6	96	278	2.9	4	3	27	9.0	0	4
1984	New Orleans	8	50	190	3.8	0	0	0	—	0	0
1985	New Orleans	16	158	643	4.1	1	6	88	14.7	0	1
Totals		**115**	**2,187**	**9,407**	**4.3**	**74**	**121**	**806**	**6.7**	**0**	**74**

*Led league

Transactions
- Selected by Houston Oilers in first round (first overall pick) of the 1978 NFL Draft;
- Traded by Oilers to New Orleans Saints for first-round pick (CB Richard Johnson) in 1985 NFL Draft (Oct. 9, 1984).

Noteworthy
- Inducted into the Pro Football Hall of Fame in 1991;
- 1979 NFL most valuable player;
- 1978–1980 NFL offensive player of the year;
- 1978 offensive rookie of the year;
- Selected to five Pro Bowls (following the 1978–1981, and 1983 seasons);
- Retired in seventh place on the NFL's all-time rushing list;
- Holds Oilers records for most career touchdown runs (73) and consecutive games with a rushing touchdown (5);
- Powered the Oilers to appearances in the 1978–79 AFC Championship Games;
- Became the first rookie since Jim Brown in 1957 to lead the NFL in rushing;
- One of his most memorable games was against the Miami Dolphins on *NFL Monday Night Football* in 1978. He rushed for 199 yards, including an 81-yard sprint, and scored 4 touchdowns to lead the Oilers to a thrilling 35–30 victory;
- His uniform number 34 is retired by the club;
- Won the Heisman Trophy as the nation's best college player as a senior at Texas;
- The Oilers traded four draft picks and tight end Jimmie Giles for the first overall selection in the 1978 NFL Draft, which they used on Campbell;
- Nicknamed "The Tyler Rose" because his hometown was Tyler, Texas;
- One of only four people who have been designated a Texas Legend by the Texas State Legislature. Davy Crockett, Sam Houston, and Stephen F. Austin are the others;
- Weighed 233 pounds, had 36-inch thighs, and still ran 40 yards in 4.6 seconds.

ROGER CRAIG (for more information, see pages 30–31)

| YR. | TEAM | G | RUSHING | | | | RECEIVING | | | | TOTAL |
			ATT	YDS	AVG	TD	REC	YDS	AVG	TD	TD
1983	San Francisco	16	176	725	4.1	8	48	427	8.9	4	12
1984	San Francisco	16	155	649	4.2	7	71	675	9.5	3	10
1985	San Francisco	16	214	1,050	4.9	9	92*	1,016	11.0	6	15
1986	San Francisco	16	204	830	4.1	7	81	624	7.7	0	7
1987	San Francisco	14	215	815	3.8	3	66	492	7.5	1	4
1988	San Francisco	16	310	1,502	4.8	9	76	534	7.0	1	10
1989	San Francisco	16	271	1,054	3.9	6	49	473	9.7	1	7
1990	San Francisco	11	141	439	3.1	1	25	201	8.0	0	1
1991	L.A. Raiders	15	162	590	3.6	1	17	136	8.0	0	1
1992	Minnesota	15	105	416	4.0	4	22	164	7.5	0	4
1993	Minnesota	14	38	119	3.1	1	19	169	8.9	1	2
Totals		**165**	**1,991**	**8,189**	**4.1**	**56**	**566**	**4,911**	**8.7**	**17**	**73**

*Led league

Transactions
- Selected by San Francisco 49ers in second round (49th pick overall) of the 1983 NFL Draft;
- Granted unconditional free agency, signed by Los Angeles Raiders (April 1, 1991);
- Granted uncondtional free agency, signed by Minnesota Vikings (March 18, 1992).

Noteworthy
- Selected to four Pro Bowls (following the 1985 and 1987–1989 seasons);
- 1988 NFL offensive player of the year;
- Helped the 49ers to victories in Super Bowls XIX, XXIII, and XXIV;
- First player to score 3 touchdowns in a Super Bowl (XIX);
- Set a 49ers postseason record by rushing for 135 yards in a 34–9 victory over Minnesota in the 1988 divisional playoffs. Also set a then-NFL postseason record with an 80-yard touchdown run in the game—the longest run of his career;
- 49ers career postseason rushing leader with 816 yards;
- First player to post 1,000 yards rushing and receiving in the same year (1985);
- Third in 49ers history with 14 100-yard rushing games;
- Finished his NFL career as the all-time leader in receptions by a running back;
- Set an NFL record for most receptions (92) by a running back in a season in 1985;
- Rushed for a career-high 190 yards against the Rams (Oct. 16, 1988);
- Longest reception was 73 yards against the Rams (Oct. 27, 1985);
- Finished his college career at Nebraska fourth on the school's career rushing list with 2,446 yards;
- Appeared as actor on the HBO series *1st and 10* and in the 1991 movie *Necessary Roughness*.

LARRY CSONKA (for more information, see pages 56–57)

YR.	TEAM	G	RUSHING ATT	YDS	AVG	TD	RECEIVING REC	YDS	AVG	TD	TOTAL TD
1968	Miami	11	138	540	3.9	6	11	118	10.7	1	7
1969	Miami	11	131	566	4.3	2	21	183	8.7	1	3
1970	Miami	14	193	874	4.5	6	11	94	8.5	0	6
1971	Miami	14	195	1,051	5.4*	7	13	113	8.7	1	8
1972	Miami	14	213	1,117	5.2	6	5	48	9.6	0	6
1973	Miami	14	219	1,003	4.6	5	7	22	3.1	0	5
1974	Miami	12	197	749	3.8	9	7	35	5.0	0	9
1975	Memphis (WFL)	7	99	421	4.3	1	5	54	10.8	1	2
1976	N.Y. Giants	12	160	569	3.6	4	6	39	6.5	0	4
1977	N.Y. Giants	14	134	464	3.5	1	2	20	10.0	0	1
1978	N.Y. Giants	14	91	311	3.4	6	7	73	10.4	0	6
1979	Miami	16	220	837	3.8	12	16	75	4.7	1	13
NFL Totals		**146**	**1,891**	**8,081**	**4.3**	**64**	**106**	**820**	**7.7**	**4**	**68**

*Led league

Transactions
- Selected by Miami Dolphins in first round (eighth overall pick) of the 1968 NFL Draft;
- Signed as free agent with New York Giants (April 7, 1976);
- Released by Giants (Feb. 1, 1979), signed as free agent with Miami Dolphins (Feb. 22, 1979).

Noteworthy
- Inducted into the Pro Football Hall of Fame in 1987;
- 1979 NFL comeback player of the year;
- Selected to five Pro Bowls (following the 1970–74 seasons);
- Helped Dolphins to three consecutive Super Bowl appearances (VI, VII, and VIII) and two victories (VII and VIII);
- Named most valuable player of Super Bowl VIII after rushing for 145 yards and 2 touchdowns in the Dolphins' 24–7 victory over Minnesota;
- Helped Dolphins become the only team in NFL history to finish a season (1972) unbeaten and untied;
- Retired in sixth place on the NFL's all-time rushing list;
- Holds Dolphins career rushing records for most yards, attempts, and touchdowns;
- Missed the 1975 NFL season after signing with the World Football League's Memphis Southmen;
- In 1972, Csonka and Mercury Morris became the first pair of running backs on the same team to rush for more than 1,000 yards in the same season;
- Nicknamed "Zonk" because of his bruising running style.

TERRELL DAVIS (for more information, see pages 32–33)

| YR. | TEAM | G | RUSHING | | | | RECEIVING | | | | TOTAL |
			ATT	YDS	AVG	TD	REC	YDS	AVG	TD	TD
1995	Denver	14	237	1,117	4.7	7	49	367	7.5	1	8
1996	Denver	16	345	1,538	4.5	13	36	310	8.6	2	15
1997	Denver	15	369	1,750	4.7	15	42	287	6.8	0	15
1998	Denver	16	392	2,008*	5.1*	21*	25	217	8.7	2	23*
1999	Denver	4	67	211	3.1	2	3	26	8.7	0	2
2000	Denver	5	78	282	3.6	2	2	4	2.0	0	2
2001	Denver	8	167	701	4.2	0	12	69	5.8	0	0
Totals		**78**	**1,655**	**7,607**	**4.6**	**60**	**169**	**1,280**	**7.6**	**5**	**65**

*Led league

Transactions

• Selected by Denver Broncos in sixth round (196th pick overall) of the 1995 NFL Draft;
• Placed on injured reserve with knee injury (Oct. 6–end of 1999 season).

Noteworthy

• Selected to the Pro Bowl three times (following the 1996–98 seasons);
• 1998 NFL most valuable player;
• 1996 and 1998 NFL offensive player of the year;
• Selected MVP of Super Bowl XXXII after rushing for 157 yards and a Super Bowl-record 3 touchdowns in Denver's 31–24 victory against Green Bay;
• Tied with Roger Craig (Super Bowl XIX), Jerry Rice (XXIV), and Ricky Watters (XXIX) for the Super Bowl single-game records for most total touchdowns in a game (3) and most points (18);
• Holds NFL postseason records for average yards per carry (5.6) and average yards per game (142.5);
• Rushed for 1,140 yards and 12 touchdowns in eight NFL postseason games;
• Averaged 97.5 rushing yards per game during career and trails only Jim Brown (104.3) and Barry Sanders (99.8) on the NFL's all-time list;
• Davis' 2,008 rushing yards in 1998 are the third most in a single season in NFL history, trailing only Eric Dickerson (2,105 in 1984) and Barry Sanders (2,053 in 1997);
• Holds or shares 56 Broncos records (21 in the postseason), including career rushing yards (7,607), rushing yards in a season (2,008), career rushing attempts (1,655), total yards from scrimmage (8,887), total touchdowns (65), career rushing touchdowns (60), and 100-yard rushing games (34);
• Rushed for a career-high 215 yards against Cincinnati (Sept. 21, 1997);
• Longest run from scrimmage was 71-yard touchdown against Baltimore (Oct. 20, 1996);
• Began his college football career as a fullback at Long Beach State and played for Pro Football Hall of Fame coach George Allen. Transferred and finished college at Georgia;
• Graduated from same high school (Lincoln High in San Diego) as Pro Football Hall of Fame running back Marcus Allen.

ERIC DICKERSON (for more information, see pages 12–13)

| | | | RUSHING | | | | RECEIVING | | | | TOTAL |
YR.	TEAM	G	ATT	YDS	AVG	TD	REC	YDS	AVG	TD	TD
1983	L.A. Rams	16	390*	1,808*	4.6	18	51	404	7.9	2	20
1984	L.A. Rams	16	379	2,105*	5.6	14*	21	139	6.6	0	14
1985	L.A. Rams	14	292	1,234	4.2	12	20	126	6.3	0	12
1986	L.A. Rams	16	404*	1,821*	4.5	11	26	205	7.9	0	11
1987	L.A. Rams	3	60	277	4.6	1	5	38	7.6	0	1
1987	Indianapolis	9	223	1,011	4.5	5	13	133	10.2	0	5
1988	Indianapolis	16	388*	1,659*	4.3	14	36	377	10.5	1	15
1989	Indianapolis	15	314	1,311	4.2	7	30	211	7.0	1	8
1990	Indianapolis	11	166	677	4.1	4	18	92	5.1	0	4
1991	Indianapolis	10	167	536	3.2	2	41	269	6.6	1	3
1992	L.A. Raiders	16	187	729	3.9	2	14	85	6.1	1	3
1993	Atlanta	2	26	91	3.5	0	6	58	9.7	0	0
Totals		**146**	**2,996**	**13,259**	**4.4**	**90**	**281**	**2,137**	**7.6**	**6**	**96**

*Led league

Transactions
- Selected by Los Angeles Rams in first round (second pick overall) of the 1983 NFL Draft;
- Traded by Rams to Indianapolis Colts for first- (WR Aaron Cox) and second-round (LB Fred Strickland) choice in the 1988 draft and second-round choice (LB Frank Stams) in the 1989 draft and RB Owen Gill. Rams also acquired a first-round choice (RB Gaston Green) in the 1988 draft and first- (RB Cleveland Gary) and second-round (CB Darryl Henley) choices in the 1989 draft and RB Greg Bell from the Buffalo Bills in exchange for Colts trading the rights to LB Cornelius Bennett to the Bills (Oct. 31, 1987);
- Traded by Colts to L.A. Raiders for fourth- (NT Anthony McCoy) and eighth-round (RB Ronald Humphrey) choices in the 1992 draft (April 26, 1992);
- Traded by Raiders to Atlanta Falcons for conditional sixth-round choice (traded) in the 1994 draft (July 7, 1993);
- Traded by Falcons to Green Bay Packers for RB John Stephens (Oct. 12, 1993). In a separate deal, the Falcons traded CB Bruce Pickens to the Packers for an undisclosed draft pick. Dickerson failed his physical and was returned to the Falcons. The Falcons kept Dickerson and agreed to trade Pickens for Stephens (Oct. 15, 1993).

Noteworthy
- Inducted into the Pro Football Hall of Fame in 1999;
- Selected to six Pro Bowls (following the 1983, 1984, 1986, and 1987–1989 seasons);
- Holds NFL single-season record for rushing yards (2,105 in 1984), and NFL postseason single-game record with 248 rushing yards against Dallas in a 1985 divisional playoff;
- Holds NFL rookie records for most rushing attempts, yards gained, and rushing touchdowns;
- His uniform number 29 is retired by the Rams.

COREY DILLON (for more information, see pages 34–35)

YR.	TEAM	G	RUSHING				RECEIVING				TOTAL
			ATT	YDS	AVG	TD	REC	YDS	AVG	TD	TD
1997	Cincinnati	16	233	1,129	4.8	10	27	259	9.6	0	10
1998	Cincinnati	15	262	1,130	4.3	4	28	178	6.4	1	5
1999	Cincinnati	15	263	1,200	4.6	5	31	290	9.4	1	6
2000	Cincinnati	16	315	1,435	4.6	7	18	158	8.8	0	7
2001	Cincinnati	16	340	1,315	3.9	10	34	228	6.7	3	13
2002	Cincinnati	16	314	1,311	4.2	7	43	298	6.9	0	7
Totals		**94**	**1,727**	**7,520**	**4.4**	**43**	**181**	**1,411**	**7.8**	**5**	**48**

Transactions
- Selected by Cincinnati Bengals in second round (43rd pick overall) of the 1997 NFL Draft.

Noteworthy
- Selected to three Pro Bowls (following the 1999–2001 seasons);
- NFL record holder for most rushing yards in a game with 278 against Denver (Oct. 22, 2000); Hall of Fame running back Walter Payton previously held the record with 275;
- All-time leading rusher in Bengals history;
- Became only fourth player in NFL history to rush for more than 1,000 yards in each of first six seasons. Eric Dickerson, Barry Sanders, and Curtis Martin are the others;
- Holds 16 Bengals records, including most rushing yards in a season (1,435 in 2000), most rushing yards in a game by a rookie (246 against Tennessee in 1997), most career 100-yard games (27), most 1,000-yard seasons (six), and most 200-yard games (3);
- Broke Jim Brown's NFL single-game rookie record for rushing yards in a game (246 yards vs. Tennessee, Dec. 4, 1997);
- Longest run from scrimmage was a Bengals' record 96 yards against Detroit (Oct. 28, 2001);
- Longest reception was 41 yards against Tampa Bay (Dec. 27, 1998);
- Played only one season at the University of Washington but set five school records, including rushing yards in a season (1,555), rushing attempts (271), rushing touchdowns (22), total touchdowns (23), all-purpose yards (2,185), and scoring (138 points);
- Named national junior college back of the year at Dixie College (St. George, Utah) before transferring to Washington;
- Excellent baseball player in high school and was selected by the San Diego Padres in the 1993 Major League Baseball draft.

TONY DORSETT

(for more information, see pages 14–15)

| YR. | TEAM | G | RUSHING | | | | RECEIVING | | | | TOTAL |
			ATT	YDS	AVG	TD	REC	YDS	AVG	TD	TD
1977	Dallas	14	208	1,007	4.8	12	29	273	9.4	1	13
1978	Dallas	16	290	1,325	4.6	7	37	378	10.2	2	10
1979	Dallas	14	250	1,107	4.4	6	45	375	8.3	1	7
1980	Dallas	15	278	1,185	4.3	11	34	263	7.7	0	11
1981	Dallas	16	342	1,646	4.8	4	32	325	10.2	2	6
1982	Dallas	9	177*	745	4.2	5	24	179	7.5	0	5
1983	Dallas	16	289	1,321	4.6	8	40	287	7.2	1	9
1984	Dallas	16	302	1,189	3.9	6	51	459	9.0	1	7
1985	Dallas	16	305	1,307	4.3	7	46	449	9.8	3	10
1986	Dallas	13	184	748	4.1	5	25	267	10.7	1	6
1987	Dallas	12	130	456	3.5	1	19	177	9.3	1	2
1988	Denver	16	181	703	3.9	5	16	122	7.6	0	5
Totals		**173**	**2,936**	**12,739**	**4.3**	**77**	**398**	**3,554**	**8.9**	**13**	**91**

*Led league

Transactions
- Selected by Dallas Cowboys in first round (second overall pick) of the 1977 NFL Draft;
- Traded by Cowboys to Denver Broncos for fifth-round (DT Jeff Roth) pick in the 1989 NFL Draft (June 3, 1988).

Noteworthy
- Inducted into the Pro Football Hall of Fame in 1994;
- 1977 NFL offensive rookie of the year;
- Selected to four Pro Bowls (following the 1978 and 1981–83 seasons);
- Retired in second place on the NFL's all-time rushing list;
- Helped Dallas defeat Denver 27–10 in Super Bowl XII;
- Played in two Super Bowls (XII and XIII) and five NFC title games;
- Set an NFL record with a 99-yard touchdown run against the Minnesota Vikings (Jan. 3, 1983);
- His 45 career 100-yard rushing games place him ninth on the NFL's all-time list;
- Set Cowboys' rookie record with 1,007 rushing yards (1977);
- Passed for 1 touchdown and recovered a fumble for a touchdown during his career;
- Cowboys traded four draft choices to Seattle for the right to select Dorsett with the second overall choice in the 1977 NFL Draft;
- Won the Heisman Trophy as the nation's best college player after his senior year at the University of Pittsburgh and was an All-America as a freshman, junior, and senior;
- Set NCAA records for rushing yards in a season (1,948 in 1976) and a career (6,082). Was first running back in college history to rush for more than 1,000 yards in all four years of eligibility.

MARSHALL FAULK (for more information, see pages 16–17)

| YR. | TEAM | G | RUSHING | | | | RECEIVING | | | | TOTAL |
			ATT	YDS	AVG	TD	REC	YDS	AVG	TD	TD
1994	Indianapolis	16	314	1,282	4.1	11	52	522	10.0	1	12
1995	Indianapolis	16	289	1,078	3.7	11	56	475	8.5	3	14
1996	Indianapolis	13	198	587	3.0	7	56	428	7.6	0	7
1997	Indianapolis	16	264	1,054	4.0	7	47	471	10.0	1	8
1998	Indianapolis	16	324	1,319	4.1	6	86	908	10.6	4	10
1999	St. Louis	16	253	1,381	5.5*	7	87	1,048	12.0	5	12
2000	St. Louis	14	253	1,359	5.4*	18*	81	830	10.2	8	26*
2001	St. Louis	14	260	1,382	5.3*	12	83	765	9.2	9	21*
2002	St. Louis	14	212	953	4.5	8	80	537	6.7	2	10
Totals		**135**	**2,367**	**10,395**	**4.4**	**87**	**628**	**5,984**	**9.5**	**33**	**120**

*Led league

Transactions

- Selected by Indianapolis Colts in the first round (second pick overall) of the 1994 NFL Draft;
- Traded by the Colts to the St. Louis Rams for second- (LB Mike Peterson) and fifth-round (DE Brad Scioli) picks in the 1999 NFL Draft (April 15, 1999).

Noteworthy

- Selected to seven Pro Bowls (following the 1995, 1996, and 1998–2002 seasons);
- Named NFL offensive player of the year in 1999, 2000, and 2001;
- Named 2000 NFL most valuable player;
- Played in two NFC Championship Games (1999 and 2001) and in Super Bowls XXXIV and XXXVI;
- Holds NFL single-season record for most touchdowns (26 in 2000);
- Faulk and Hall of Fame running back Eric Dickerson are only two players in league history to rush for more than 5,000 yards for two different teams;
- Faulk and Emmitt Smith are only two players in league history to score more than 20 touchdowns in consecutive seasons;
- In 2002, moved past Hall of Fame running back Tony Dorsett and into seventh place on the NFL's career yards from scrimmage list;
- Holds Rams' all-time record for touchdowns;
- First NFL player to gain more than 2,000 yards from scrimmage in four consecutive seasons;
- Longest run from scrimmage was 71-yard touchdown against Carolina (Nov. 11, 2001);
- Longest reception was 85-yard touchdown catch against Washington (Oct. 23, 1994);
- Rushed for a career-high 220 yards against New Orleans (Dec. 24, 2000);
- Gained a career-high 204 receiving yards against Chicago (Dec. 26, 1999);
- Has converted 4 two-point conversions during his career;
- All-America running back three times at San Diego State.

CHUCK FOREMAN (for more information, see pages 36–37)

| YR. | TEAM | G | RUSHING | | | | RECEIVING | | | | TOTAL |
			ATT	YDS	AVG	TD	REC	YDS	AVG	TD	TD
1973	Minnesota	12	182	801	4.4	4	37	362	9.8	2	6
1974	Minnesota	13	199	777	3.9	9	53	586	11.1	6	15*
1975	Minnesota	14	280	1,070	3.8	13	73*	691	9.5	9	22
1976	Minnesota	14	278	1,155	4.2	13	55	567	10.3	1	14*
1977	Minnesota	14	270	1,112	4.1	6	38	308	8.1	3	9
1978	Minnesota	14	237	749	3.2	5	61	396	6.5	2	7
1979	Minnesota	12	87	223	2.6	2	19	147	7.7	0	2
1980	New England	16	23	63	2.7	1	14	99	7.1	0	1
Totals		**109**	**1,556**	**5,950**	**3.8**	**53**	**350**	**3,156**	**9.0**	**23**	**76**

*Led league

Transactions
- Selected by Minnesota Vikings in first round (12th overall pick) of the 1973 NFL Draft;
- Traded by Vikings to New England Patriots for a third-round (T Tim Irwin) pick in 1981 NFL Draft (April 17, 1980).

Noteworthy
- Selected to five Pro Bowls (following the 1973–77 seasons);
- 1973 NFL offensive rookie of the year;
- Finished his NFL career as the Minnesota Vikings' all-time leader in rushing yards (5,887) and receptions (336);
- Helped power the Vikings to six consecutive NFC Central Division titles (1973–78), four NFC Championship Games (1973, 1974, 1976, and 1977), and three Super Bowl appearances (VIII, IX, and XI) during his seven-year career in Minnesota;
- Holds Vikings' records for most touchdowns in a season (22), most rushing yards in a rookie season (801), and most consecutive seasons (6 from 1973–78) leading the team in combined rushing and receiving yards;
- Holds Vikings' records for most rushing yards in a game—a career-high 200 against the Eagles on Oct. 24, 1976—and most combined rushing and receiving yards in a game (265 in the same game as his rushing mark);
- Set a career-high with 118 receiving yards against the Giants (Oct. 17, 1976);
- Played running back and wide receiver at the University of Miami and finished as the school's all-time leading rusher for a season and career;
- Son, Jay, has played linebacker for the Buffalo Bills and Houston Texans.

CHARLIE GARNER (for more information, see pages 74–75)

| YR. | TEAM | G | RUSHING | | | | RECEIVING | | | | TOTAL |
			ATT	YDS	AVG	TD	REC	YDS	AVG	TD	TD
1994	Philadelphia	10	109	399	3.7	3	8	74	9.3	0	3
1995	Philadelphia	15	108	588	5.4*	6	10	61	6.1	0	6
1996	Philadelphia	15	66	346	5.2	1	14	92	6.6	0	1
1997	Philadelphia	16	116	547	4.7	3	24	225	9.4	0	3
1998	Philadelphia	10	96	381	4.0	4	19	110	5.8	0	4
1999	San Francisco	16	241	1,229	5.1	4	56	535	9.6	2	6
2000	San Francisco	16	258	1,142	4.4	7	68	647	9.5	3	10
2001	Oakland	16	211	839	4.0	1	72	578	8.0	2	3
2002	Oakland	16	182	962	5.3	7	91	941	10.3	4	11
Totals		**130**	**1,387**	**6,433**	**4.6**	**36**	**362**	**3,263**	**9.0**	**11**	**47**

*Led league

Transactions
- Selected by Philadelphia Eagles in the second round (42nd pick overall) of the 1994 NFL Draft;
- On injured reserve with rib injury (December 10–end of 1998 season);
- Released by Eagles (April 20, 1999), signed by San Francisco 49ers (July 19, 1999);
- Granted unconditional free agency (March 2, 2001), signed by Oakland Raiders (April 13, 2001).

Noteworthy
- Selected to one Pro Bowl (following the 2000 season);
- Set single-season Raiders record for most receptions by a running back (91 in 2002);
- Returned 35 kickoffs for 707 yards for career;
- Rushed for a career-high 201 yards against Dallas (Sept. 24, 2000);
- Totaled a career-high 91 receiving yards against Denver (Dec. 22, 2002);
- Longest run from scrimmage was 55 yards against Washington (Oct. 8, 1995);
- Longest reception was 69 yards against Buffalo (Oct. 6, 2002);
- Set national junior college record for most rushing yards in a game (430) while playing at Scottsdale Community College in Arizona;
- Selected as Virginia high school football player of the year as a senior at Jeb Stuart High.

EDDIE GEORGE (for more information, see pages 38–39)

			RUSHING				RECEIVING				TOTAL
YR.	TEAM	G	ATT	YDS	AVG	TD	REC	YDS	AVG	TD	TD
1996	Houston	16	335	1,368	4.1	8	23	182	7.9	0	8
1997	Tennessee	16	357	1,399	3.9	6	7	44	6.3	1	7
1998	Tennessee	16	348	1,294	3.7	5	37	310	8.4	1	6
1999	Tennessee	16	320	1,304	4.1	9	47	458	9.7	4	13
2000	Tennessee	16	403*	1,509	3.7	14	50	453	9.1	2	16
2001	Tennessee	16	315	939	3.0	5	37	279	7.5	0	5
2002	Tennessee	16	343	1,165	3.4	12	36	255	7.1	2	14
Totals		**112**	**2,421**	**8,978**	**3.7**	**59**	**237**	**1,981**	**8.4**	**10**	**69**

*Led league

Transactions
- Selected by Houston Oilers in the first round (14th pick overall) of the 1996 NFL Draft;
- Oilers franchise moved to Tennessee in 1997 and was renamed Titans in 1999.

Noteworthy
- Selected to four Pro Bowls (following the 1997–2000 seasons);
- Played in two AFC Championship Games (1999 and 2002) and in Super Bowl XXXIV;
- Only running back in NFL history to post more than 300 carries in each of his first six seasons;
- In 2002, surpassed Hall of Fame running back Earl Campbell to become the leading rusher in franchise history;
- In seven career playoff games, he has gained 640 yards on 165 carries and scored 5 touchdowns;
- Rushed for a postseason career-high 162 yards against Indianapolis in a 1999 AFC Divisional Playoff Game;
- Rushed for a career-high 216 yards against Oakland (Aug. 31, 1997);
- Longest run from scrimmage was 76 yards against Jacksonville (Sept. 8, 1996);
- Longest reception was a 54-yard touchdown catch against San Francisco (Oct. 3, 1999);
- George's streak of 112 games started (through 2002), trails only Walter Payton (170) and Ricky Watters (114) for most ever by a running back in NFL history;
- Won the Heisman Trophy and Maxwell Award as the nation's best college player after senior year at Ohio State University in 1995;
- Joined Billy Cannon, Earl Campbell, and Mike Rozier as Heisman Trophy-winning running backs who were drafted by the Oilers/Titans franchise;
- Won Doak Walker Award as nation's best college running back in 1995.

RED GRANGE (for more information, see pages 76–77)

| YR. | TEAM | G | RUSHING | | | | RECEIVING | | | | TOTAL |
			ATT	YDS	AVG	TD	REC	YDS	AVG	TD	TD
1925	Chicago Bears	5	n/a	n/a	n/a	2	n/a	n/a	n/a	n/a	3
1926	N.Y. Yankees (AFL)	15	n/a	n/a	n/a	n/a	n/a	n/a	n/a	n/a	8
1927	N.Y. Yankees	13	n/a	n/a	n/a	1	n/a	n/a	n/a	n/a	1
1928	DID NOT PLAY										
1929	Chicago Bears	14	n/a	n/a	n/a	2	n/a	n/a	n/a	n/a	2
1930	Chicago Bears	14	n/a	n/a	n/a	6	n/a	n/a	n/a	2	8
1931	Chicago Bears	13	n/a	n/a	n/a	5	n/a	n/a	n/a	2	7
1932	Chicago Bears	12	57	136	2.4	3	11	168	15.3	4	7*
1933	Chicago Bears	13	81	277	3.4	1	3	74	24.7	0	1
1934	Chicago Bears	12	32	156	4.9	1	2	46	23.0	2	3
NFL Totals		**96**	**170**	**569**	**3.3**	**21**	**16**	**288**	**18.0**	**10**	**32**

*Led league

Transactions
• Signed as free agent with Chicago Bears in 1925;
• Signed as free agent with New York Yankees in 1927;
• Signed as free agent with Chicago Bears in 1929.

Noteworthy
• Charter enshrinee of the Pro Football Hall of Fame in 1963;
• In 1925, NFL teams were fortunate to draw 10,000 fans to a game. Grange was the first NFL gate attraction—the Bears drew 39,000 fans to his first game, and the Bears game in New York against the Giants 10 days later attracted a record crowd of 68,000.
• Completed 24 of 71 career NFL pass attempts for 346 yards and 10 touchdowns; also intercepted a pass and returned it for a touchdown and scored 2 extra points;
• Nicknamed the "Galloping Ghost";
• Bears won the 1932 and 1933 NFL titles, and played in the 1934 NFL Championship Game, but lost the famed "Sneakers Game";
• Also was an excellent defensive player for the Bears;
• Suffered a knee injury in 1927 that forced him to miss the 1928 season;
• His uniform number 77 is retired by the Bears;
• All-America player in college at the University of Illinois;
• Sold insurance door to door during the offseason;
• Given name is Harold.

AHMAN GREEN (for more information, see pages 98–99)

| YR. | TEAM | G | RUSHING | | | | RECEIVING | | | | TOTAL |
			ATT	YDS	AVG	TD	REC	YDS	AVG	TD	TD
1998	Seattle	16	35	209	6.0	1	3	2	0.7	0	1
1999	Seattle	14	26	120	4.6	0	0	0	0.0	0	0
2000	Green Bay	16	263	1,175	4.5	10	73	559	7.7	3	13
2001	Green Bay	16	304	1,387	4.6	9	62	594	9.6	2	11
2002	Green Bay	14	286	1,240	4.3	7	57	393	6.9	2	9
Totals		**76**	**914**	**4,131**	**4.5**	**27**	**195**	**1,548**	**7.9**	**7**	**34**

Transactions
- Selected by Seattle Seahawks in third round (76th pick overall) of the 1998 NFL Draft;
- Traded by the Seahawks with fifth-round choice (WR Joey Jamison) in 2000 NFL Draft to Green Bay Packers for CB Fred Vinson and sixth-round choice (DT Tim Watson) in 2000 draft (April 14, 2000).

Noteworthy
- Selected to three Pro Bowls (following the 2000–02 seasons);
- In 2002, joined Jim Taylor (1960–64) and John Brockington (1971–73) as only running backs in Packers' history to rush for more than 1,000 yards in three consecutive seasons;
- Joined Edgar Bennett (1993–95) as only running backs in Packers' history to catch more than 50 passes in three consecutive seasons;
- Green's 14 career 100-yard rushing games through 2002 rank second in Packers' history behind Taylor (26);
- Led Green Bay in rushing and receiving in 2000 and 2001. Only running back in team history to accomplish such a feat;
- Longest run from scrimmage was for an 83-yard touchdown against Detroit (Sept. 9, 2001);
- Longest reception was 42 yards against Jacksonville (Dec. 3, 2001);
- Has 63 career kickoffs for 1,438 yards (22.8-yard average);
- Helped the University of Nebraska win the 1997 national championship with an Orange Bowl victory over Tennessee;
- Nebraska high school player of the year as senior at Central High in Omaha;
- Nickname is "Batman"; Has a Batman tattoo and owns an extensive collection of comic books and posters of the superhero.

FRANCO HARRIS (for more information, see pages 18–19)

| YR. | TEAM | G | RUSHING | | | | RECEIVING | | | | TOTAL |
			ATT	YDS	AVG	TD	REC	YDS	AVG	TD	TD
1972	Pittsburgh	14	188	1,055	5.6	10	21	180	8.6	1	11
1973	Pittsburgh	12	188	698	3.7	3	10	69	6.9	0	3
1974	Pittsburgh	12	208	1,006	4.8	5	23	200	8.7	1	6
1975	Pittsburgh	14	262	1,246	4.8	10	28	214	7.6	1	11
1976	Pittsburgh	14	289	1,128	3.9	14*	23	151	6.6	0	14*
1977	Pittsburgh	14	300	1,162	3.9	11	11	62	5.6	0	11
1978	Pittsburgh	16	310	1,082	3.5	8	22	144	6.5	0	8
1979	Pittsburgh	15	267	1,186	4.4	11	36	291	8.1	1	12
1980	Pittsburgh	13	208	789	3.8	4	30	196	6.5	2	6
1981	Pittsburgh	16	242	987	4.1	8	37	250	6.8	1	9
1982	Pittsburgh	9	140	604	4.3	2	31	249	8.0	0	2
1983	Pittsburgh	16	279	1,007	3.6	5	34	278	8.2	2	7
1984	Seattle	8	68	170	2.5	0	1	3	3.0	0	0
Totals		**173**	**2,949**	**12,120**	**4.1**	**91**	**307**	**2,287**	**7.4**	**9**	**100**

*Led league

Transactions
- Selected by Pittsburgh Steelers in first round (13th overall pick) of the 1972 NFL Draft;
- Released by Steelers (Aug. 20, 1984), signed as free agent with Seattle Seahawks (Sept. 5, 1984).

Noteworthy
- Inducted into the Pro Football Hall of Fame in 1990;
- 1972 NFL offensive rookie of the year;
- Selected to nine Pro Bowls (following the 1972–1980 seasons);
- Retired in third place on the NFL's all-time rushing list;
- His "Immaculate Reception" provided the game-winning points in the Steelers' 1972 divisional playoff game against Oakland. It was the first postseason victory in Steelers' history;
- Helped Steelers win eight AFC Central titles and four Super Bowls (IX, X, XIII, and XIV);
- Set a then-Super Bowl record by rushing for 158 yards and a touchdown in the Steelers' 16–6 victory over Minnesota in Super Bowl X. Was named the game's most valuable player;
- Holds Super Bowl career rushing records for most yards (354) and attempts (101);
- Holds the NFL postseason rushing record for most attempts (400) and held the postseason record for most yards (1,556) until Emmitt Smith broke the record (1,586) in 1999;
- Held or shared 24 NFL records when he retired;
- Steelers all-time leading rusher and totaled a franchise-best 47 100-yard rushing games;
- Son of a U.S. serviceman, had fan club in Pittsburgh called "Franco's Army."

TRAVIS HENRY (for more information, see pages 100–101)

| YR. | TEAM | G | RUSHING | | | | RECEIVING | | | | TOTAL |
			ATT	YDS	AVG	TD	REC	YDS	AVG	TD	TD
2001	Buffalo	13	213	729	3.4	4	22	179	8.1	0	4
2002	Buffalo	16	325	1,438	4.4	13	43	309	7.2	1	14
Totals		**29**	**538**	**2,167**	**4.0**	**17**	**65**	**488**	**7.5**	**1**	**18**

Transactions
• Selected by Buffalo Bills in second round (58th pick overall) of the 2001 NFL Draft.

Noteworthy
• Selected to one Pro Bowl (following the 2002 season);
• First Bills running back to score at least 13 rushing touchdowns in a season since O.J. Simpson in 1975;
• Ran for 1,438 yards in 2002, fifth-highest total in franchise history;
• Tied with Ricky Williams of Miami for most 125-yard games (6) in 2002;
• Rushed for a career-high 159 yards against Houston (Oct. 13, 2002);
• Longest run was 34 yards against Miami (Oct. 20, 2002);
• Longest reception was a 26-yard touchdown catch against Chicago (Sept. 29, 2002);
• All-time leading rusher at the University of Tennesse with 3,078 yards;
• All-America high school running back as selected by *Parade* magazine;
• Named "Mr. Florida Football" as senior at Frostproof High.

PRIEST HOLMES (for more information, see pages 102–103)

| YR. | TEAM | G | RUSHING | | | | RECEIVING | | | | TOTAL |
			ATT	YDS	AVG	TD	REC	YDS	AVG	TD	TD
1997	Baltimore	7	0	0	0.0	0	0	0	0.0	0	0
1998	Baltimore	16	233	1,008	4.3	7	43	260	6.0	0	7
1999	Baltimore	9	89	506	5.7	1	13	104	8.0	1	2
2000	Baltimore	16	137	588	4.3	2	32	221	6.9	0	2
2001	Kansas City	16	327	1,555*	4.8	8	62	614	9.9	2	10
2002	Kansas City	14	313	1,615	5.2	21*	70	672	9.6	3	24*
Totals		**78**	**1,099**	**5,272**	**4.8**	**39**	**220**	**1,871**	**8.5**	**6**	**45**

*Led league

Transactions
- Signed with Baltimore Ravens as undrafted free agent (April, 25, 1997);
- Granted unconditional free agency, signed by Kansas City Chiefs (April 1, 2000).

Noteworthy
- Selected to two Pro Bowls (following the 2001 and 2002 seasons);
- 2002 NFL offensive player of the year;
- Named Chiefs MVP in 2001 and 2002;
- First running back in Chiefs history to rush for more than 1,000 yards in consecutive seasons;
- Set 23 Chiefs records in 2002;
- Rushing and total touchdown totals from 2002 tie for third-most ever in an NFL season;
- Returned 4 kickoffs for 51 yards for career;
- Rushed for a career-high 227 yards against Cincinnati (Nov. 22, 1998);
- Longest run from scrimmage was 72 yards against Tennessee (Dec. 5, 1999);
- Longest reception was 67 yards against Oakland (Dec. 9, 2001);
- Has recorded 7 career tackles on special teams;
- Rushed for 120 yards to help University of Texas upset Nebraska in 1996 Big 12 Championship Game.

PAUL HORNUNG (for more information, see pages 78–79)

| YR. | TEAM | G | RUSHING | | | | RECEIVING | | | | TOTAL |
			ATT	YDS	AVG	TD	REC	YDS	AVG	TD	TD
1957	Green Bay	12	60	319	5.3*	3	6	34	5.7	0	3
1958	Green Bay	12	69	310	4.5	2	15	137	9.1	0	2
1959	Green Bay	12	152	681	4.5	7	15	113	7.5	0	7
1960	Green Bay	12	160	671	4.2	13*	28	257	9.2	2	15*
1961	Green Bay	12	127	597	4.7	8	15	145	9.7	2	10
1962	Green Bay	9	57	219	3.8	5	9	168	18.7	2	7
1963			DID NOT PLAY								
1964	Green Bay	14	103	415	4.0	5	9	98	10.9	0	5
1965	Green Bay	12	89	299	3.4	5	19	336	17.7	3	8
1966	Green Bay	9	76	200	2.6	2	14	192	13.7	3	5
Totals		**104**	**893**	**3,711**	**4.2**	**50**	**130**	**1,480**	**11.4**	**12**	**62**

*Led league

Transactions
- Selected by Green Bay Packers in first round (first overall pick) of the 1957 NFL Draft;
- Selected by New Orleans Saints in 1967 expansion draft, but did not play for Saints.

Noteworthy
- Inducted into the Pro Football Hall of Fame in 1986;
- 1961 NFL most valuable player;
- Selected to two Pro Bowls (following the 1959 and 1960 seasons);
- Set league record by scoring 176 points (15 touchdowns, 15 field goals, and 41 extra points) in only 12 games (1960);
- Part of Packers' four NFL Championship Game victories (1961, 1962, 1965, and 1966) and defeat of Kansas City Chiefs in Super Bowl I. Also played in the 1960 NFL Championship Game;
- Tied then-postseason record by scoring 19 points (1 touchdown, 3 field goals, and 4 extra points) in the Packers' 37–0 victory over the Giants in 1961;
- Completed 24 of 55 career pass attempts for 383 yards and 5 touchdowns;
- Scored 760 career points (66 field goals, 190 extra points, and 62 touchdowns);
- Led NFL in scoring three consecutive seasons (94 points in 1959, 176 in 1960, and 146 in 1961);
- Was the first winner of the Heisman Trophy, given to the nation's best college player, to come from a losing team. His 1956 Notre Dame team finished the season 2–8;
- As the Fighting Irish quarterback in 1956, he led the team in passing, rushing, kickoff returns, punting, and scoring. He also finished second on the team in punt returns, tackles, and interceptions;
- Nicknamed "The Golden Boy" because of his blonde hair and good looks.

Bo Jackson

(for more information, see pages 80–81)

| Yr. | Team | G | RUSHING | | | | RECEIVING | | | | Total |
			Att	Yds	Avg	TD	Rec	Yds	Avg	TD	TD
1987	L.A. Raiders	7	81	554	6.8	4	16	136	8.5	2	6
1988	L.A. Raiders	10	136	580	4.3	3	9	79	8.8	0	3
1989	L.A. Raiders	11	173	950	5.5	4	9	69	7.7	0	4
1990	L.A. Raiders	10	125	698	5.6	5	6	68	11.3	0	5
Totals		**38**	**515**	**2,782**	**5.4**	**16**	**40**	**352**	**8.8**	**2**	**18**

Transactions

• Selected by Tampa Bay Buccaneers in first round (first pick overall) of the 1986 NFL Draft. On reserve/did not sign list for the entire 1986 NFL season;
• Selected by the Los Angeles Raiders in seventh round (183rd pick overall) of the 1987 NFL Draft;
• On reserve/did not report list (Aug. 27–Oct. 24, 1987);
• On reserve/did not report list (Aug. 22–Oct. 12, 1988);
• On reserve/did not report list (July 21–Oct. 11, 1989);
• On reserve/did not report list (July 27–Oct. 21, 1990).

Noteworthy

• Selected to play in one Pro Bowl (following the 1990 season);
• Also played in the 1989 in the Major League Baseball All-Star Game. Only player in sports history to appear in both a Pro Bowl and All-Star game;
• Set Raiders single-game record with 221 rushing yards against Seattle on *NFL Monday Night Football*, (Nov. 30, 1987);
• Longest run from scrimmage was a Raiders' record 92-yard touchdown (vs. Cincinnati, Nov. 5, 1989);
• Decided to play professional baseball rather than sign with the Tampa Bay Buccaneers in 1986;
• Played for Major League Baseball's Kansas City Royals (1986–1990), Chicago White Sox (1991 and 1993) and California Angels (1994);
• In 2,393 career Major League Baseball at-bats, hit for a .250 average with 598 hits, 86 doubles, 14 triples, 141 home runs, and 415 runs batted in;
• Finished fourth in the major leagues with 32 home runs and 105 RBI (1989);
• Won Heisman Trophy as nation's best college football player after rushing for 1,786 yards and 17 touchdowns as senior at Auburn University in 1985;
• Consensus first-team All-America in 1983 and 1985;
• Two-time Alabama state high school decathlon champion at McAdory High in McCalla, Alabama;
• Set Alabama state high school records 60- and 100-yard sprints, 60- and 120-yard hurdles, long jump, and high jump;
• Real name is Vincent Edward Jackson.

EDGERRIN JAMES (for more information, see pages 104–105)

| YR. | TEAM | G | RUSHING | | | | RECEIVING | | | | TOTAL |
			ATT	YDS	AVG	TD	REC	YDS	AVG	TD	TD
1999	Indianapolis	16	369*	1,553*	4.2	13	62	586	9.5	4	17
2000	Indianapolis	16	387	1,709*	4.4	13	63	594	9.4	5	18
2001	Indianapolis	6	151	662	4.4	3	24	193	8.0	0	3
2002	Indianapolis	15	277	989	3.6	2	61	354	5.8	1	3
Totals		**53**	**1,184**	**4,913**	**4.2**	**31**	**210**	**1,727**	**8.2**	**10**	**41**

*Led league

Transactions
- Selected by the Indianapolis Colts in first round (fourth pick overall) of the 1999 NFL Draft;
- Placed on injured reserve with knee injury (Nov. 21–end of 2001 season).

Noteworthy
- Selected to two Pro Bowls (following the 1999–2000 seasons);
- 1999 NFL offensive rookie of the year;
- Set a Colts single-season record with 1,709 rushing yards in 2000;
- Joined Eric Dickerson (1983–84), Earl Campbell (1978–79), Jim Brown (1957–58), and Bill Paschal (1943–44) as the only players in NFL history to lead the league in rushing in each of their first two seasons;
- James and Eric Dickerson are the only players in NFL history to gain more than 4,000 total yards from scrimmage in their first two seasons;
- Holds NFL record for most 100-yard rushing games (10) in a rookie season;
- Set career-high with 219 rushing yards against Seattle (Oct. 15, 2000);
- Longest run from scrimmage was 72 yards against the New York Giants (Nov. 14, 1999);
- Longest reception was 60 yards against Jacksonville (Sept. 25, 2000);
- All-time leader in University of Miami history with 14 100-yard rushing games;
- Set Miami single-season rushing records for yards (1,416) and touchdowns (17) as junior in 1998;
- Set Miami single-game record with 299 rushing yards against UCLA in 1998;
- Only player in Miami history to rush for more than 1,000 yards in consecutive seasons (1997–98);
- All-America running back as senior at Immokalee High School in Florida.

JOHN HENRY JOHNSON (for more information, see pages 58–59)

| YR. | TEAM | G | RUSHING | | | | RECEIVING | | | | TOTAL |
			ATT	YDS	AVG	TD	REC	YDS	AVG	TD	TD
1954	San Francisco	12	129	681	5.3	9	28	183	6.5	0	9
1955	San Francisco	7	19	69	3.6	1	2	6	3.0	0	1
1956	San Francisco	12	80	301	3.8	2	8	90	11.3	0	2
1957	Detroit	12	129	621	4.8	5	20	141	7.1	0	5
1958	Detroit	9	56	254	4.5	0	7	60	8.6	0	0
1959	Detroit	10	82	270	3.3	2	7	34	4.9	1	3
1960	Pittsburgh	12	118	621	5.3	2	12	112	9.3	1	3
1961	Pittsburgh	14	213	787	3.7	6	24	262	10.9	1	7
1962	Pittsburgh	14	251	1,141	4.5	7	32	226	7.1	2	9
1963	Pittsburgh	12	186	773	4.2	4	21	145	6.9	1	5
1964	Pittsburgh	14	235	1,048	4.5	7	17	69	4.1	1	8
1965	Pittsburgh	1	3	11	3.7	0	0	0	—	0	0
1966	Houston	14	70	226	3.2	3	8	150	18.8	0	3
Totals		**143**	**1,571**	**6,803**	**4.3**	**48**	**186**	**1,478**	**7.9**	**7**	**55**

Transactions

- Selected by Pittsburgh Steelers in second round (18th pick overall) of the 1953 NFL Draft;
- Did not sign with Pittsburgh and played for Calgary Stampeders in Canadian Western Interprovincial Football Union during 1953 season;
- Traded by Steelers to San Francisco 49ers for HB Ed Fullerton (1954);
- Traded by 49ers with seventh-round (CB Ralph Pfeifer) draft pick in 1958 NFL Draft to Detroit Lions for HB Bill Stits (1957);
- Traded by Lions to Pittsburgh Steelers for fourth-round (T Roger Brown) pick in 1960 NFL Draft and third-round (T Dick Mills) selection in 1961 draft;
- Signed as free agent by Houston in 1966.

Noteworthy

- Inducted into the Pro Football Hall of Fame in 1987;
- Selected to four Pro Bowls (following the 1954 and 1962–64 seasons);
- Member of the 49ers' "Million Dollar Backfield" with quarterback Y.A. Tittle, running back Hugh McElhenny, and fullback Joe Perry;
- Named most valuable player of the Western Interprovincial Football Union while playing for Calgary Stampeders in Canada during 1953 season;
- Originally attended St. Mary's College (Calif.) and played three years (1949–1951) before program was disbanded. Transferred to Arizona State and was named All-Border Conference in 1952.

LEROY KELLY (for more information, see pages 40–41)

YR.	TEAM	G	RUSHING				RECEIVING				TOTAL
			ATT	YDS	AVG	TD	REC	YDS	AVG	TD	TD
1964	Cleveland	14	6	12	2.0	0	0	0	0.0	—	1
1965	Cleveland	13	37	139	3.8	0	9	122	13.6	0	2
1966	Cleveland	14	209	1,141	5.5*	15*	32	366	11.4	1	16*
1967	Cleveland	14	235*	1,205*	5.1*	11*	20	282	14.1	2	13
1968	Cleveland	14	248*	1,239*	5.0	16*	22	297	13.5	4	20*
1969	Cleveland	13	196	817	4.2	9	20	267	13.4	1	10
1970	Cleveland	13	206	656	3.2	6	24	311	13.0	2	8
1971	Cleveland	14	234	865	3.7	10	25	252	10.1	2	12
1972	Cleveland	14	224	811	3.6	4	23	204	8.9	1	5
1973	Cleveland	13	132	389	2.9	3	15	180	12.0	0	3
Totals		**136**	**1,727**	**7,274**	**4.2**	**74**	**190**	**2,281**	**12.0**	**13**	**90**

*Led league

Transactions
• Selected by Cleveland Browns in eighth round (110th overall pick) of the 1964 NFL Draft.

Noteworthy
• Inducted into the Pro Football Hall of Fame in 1994;
• Selected to six consecutive Pro Bowls (following the 1966–1971 seasons);
• Retired in fourth place on the NFL's all-time rushing list;
• Spent first two NFL seasons mainly as kick returner and backup to Jim Brown;
• Led the NFL in punt-return average (15.6 yards per return) and punt-return touchdowns (2) in 1965;
• Returned 94 punts for 990 yards (10.5-yard average) and 3 touchdowns, and 76 kickoffs for 1,784 yards (23.5-yard average) during his career;
• Played in the 1965, 1968, and 1969 NFL Championship Games and led the Browns to the playoffs three other times (1967, 1971, and 1972);
• Longest run from scrimmage was a 70-yard touchdown against Atlanta (Oct. 30, 1966);
• Completed 3 of 16 career pass attempts for 93 yards and 2 touchdowns. Also punted 10 times for 407 yards (40.7-yard average).

JAMAL LEWIS

(for more information, see pages 106–107)

| YR. | TEAM | G | RUSHING | | | | RECEIVING | | | | TOTAL |
			ATT	YDS	AVG	TD	REC	YDS	AVG	TD	TD
2000	Baltimore	16	309	1,364	4.4	6	27	296	11.0	0	6
2001	Baltimore	DID NOT PLAY—INJURED									
2002	Baltimore	16	308	1,327	4.3	6	47	442	9.4	1	7
Totals		**32**	**617**	**2,691**	**4.4**	**12**	**74**	**738**	**10.0**	**1**	**13**

*Led league

Transactions

- Selected by Baltimore Ravens in the first round (fifth pick overall) of the 2000 NFL Draft;
- On injured reserve with knee injury (Aug. 28–end of 2001 season).

Noteworthy

- Set Ravens rookie record for rushing yards in 2000;
- Lewis and Pro Football Hall of Fame running back Tony Dorsett are only players in NFL history to rush for 1,000 yards as rookies and help lead respective teams to Super Bowl victory;
- Became Ravens' all-time rushing leader in 2002;
- Rushed for 338 yards and 4 touchdowns during the 2000 NFL playoffs;
- Twice has rushed for a career-high 187 yards in a game (vs. Cleveland, Oct. 6, 2002; and vs. Dallas, Nov. 19, 2000);
- Longest run from scrimmage was franchise record 75-yard effort against Cleveland (Oct. 6, 2002);
- Longest reception was 77-yard touchdown catch against New Orleans (Dec. 8, 2002);
- *AP* SEC freshman of the year at University of Tennessee.

CURTIS MARTIN (for more information, see pages 42–43)

| YR. | TEAM | G | RUSHING | | | | RECEIVING | | | | TOTAL |
			ATT	YDS	AVG	TD	REC	YDS	AVG	TD	TD
1995	New England	16	368	1,487	4.0	14	30	261	8.7	1	15
1996	New England	16	316	1,152	3.6	14	46	333	7.2	3	17
1997	New England	13	274	1,160	4.2	4	41	296	7.2	1	5
1998	N.Y. Jets	15	369	1,287	3.5	8	43	365	8.5	1	9
1999	N.Y. Jets	16	367	1,464	4.0	5	45	259	5.8	0	5
2000	N.Y. Jets	16	316	1,204	3.8	9	70	508	7.3	2	11
2001	N.Y. Jets	16	333	1,513	4.5	10	53	320	6.0	0	10
2002	N.Y. Jets	16	261	1,094	4.2	7	49	362	7.4	0	7
Totals		**124**	**2,604**	**10,361**	**4.0**	**71**	**376**	**2,704**	**7.2**	**8**	**79**

Transactions
- Selected by New England Patriots in the third round (74th pick overall) of the 1995 NFL Draft;
- Granted restricted free agency, signed by N.Y. Jets (March 20, 1998).

Noteworthy
- Selected to four Pro Bowls (following the 1995, 1996, 1998, and 2001 seasons);
- Helped lead Patriots to appearance in Super Bowl XXXI;
- Martin and Barry Sanders are only running backs in NFL history to rush for more than 1,000 yards in each of their first eight seasons;
- Became sixteenth player in NFL history to rush for more than 10,000 career yards;
- Holds Jets record for most career 100-yard games (29);
- Has gained 578 rushing yards and scored 8 touchdowns in seven NFL postseason games;
- Finished second in the league in rushing in 2001;
- Rushed for career-high 203 yards against Indianapolis (Dec. 3, 2000);
- Longest run from scrimmage was 70-yard touchdown against Chicago (Sept. 21, 1997);
- Longest reception was 41 yards against Miami (Nov. 3, 1996);
- Set Jets' single-season rushing record with 1,513 yards in 2001;
- Completed 2 of 2 career passes for 36 yards and 2 touchdowns.

OLLIE MATSON (for more information, see pages 82–83)

| YR. | TEAM | G | RUSHING | | | | RECEIVING | | | | TOTAL |
			ATT	YDS	AVG	TD	REC	YDS	AVG	TD	TD
1952	Chicago Cardinals	12	96	344	3.6	3	11	187	17.0	3	9
1953	Chicago Cardinals	DID NOT PLAY—MILITARY SERVICE									
1954	Chicago Cardinals	12	101	506	5.0	4	34	611	18.0	3	9
1955	Chicago Cardinals	12	109	475	4.4	1	17	237	13.9	2	5
1956	Chicago Cardinals	12	192	924	4.8	5	15	199	13.3	2	8
1957	Chicago Cardinals	12	134	577	4.3	6	20	451	22.6	3	9
1958	Chicago Cardinals	12	129	505	3.9	5	33	465	14.1	3	10
1959	L.A. Rams	12	161	863	5.4	6	18	130	7.2	0	6
1960	L.A. Rams	12	61	170	2.8	1	15	98	6.5	0	1
1961	L.A. Rams	14	24	181	7.5	2	29	537	18.5	3	5
1962	L.A. Rams	13	3	0	0.0	0	3	49	16.3	1	1
1963	Detroit	8	13	20	1.5	0	2	20	10.0	0	0
1964	Philadelphia	12	96	404	4.2	4	17	242	14.2	1	5
1965	Philadelphia	14	22	103	4.7	2	2	29	14.5	1	3
1966	Philadelphia	14	29	101	3.5	1	6	30	5.0	1	2
Totals		**171**	**1,170**	**5,173**	**4.4**	**40**	**222**	**3,285**	**14.8**	**23**	**73**

Transactions

- Selected by Chicago Cardinals in first round (third overall pick) of the 1952 NFL Draft;
- On March 23, 1959 traded by the Chicago Cardinals to the Los Angeles Rams for T Frank Fuller, DE Glenn Holtzman, T Ken Panfil, DT Art Hauser, E John Tracey, FB Larry Hickman, HB Don Brown, the Rams' second-round choice in 1960, and a player to be delivered during the 1959 training camp. Tied for the fifth largest trade in NFL history;
- Traded by the Rams to the Detroit Lions in August, 1962;
- Traded by Lions with DT Floyd Peters to Philadelphia Eagles for T J.D. Smith (1964).

Noteworthy

- Inducted into the Pro Football Hall of Fame in 1972;
- Selected to six Pro Bowls (following the 1952 and 1954–58 seasons);
- First player in NFL history to surpass 10,000 total yards from scrimmage;
- Returned 65 punts for 595 yards (9.2 yards per return) and 3 touchdowns, and 143 kickoffs for 3,746 yards (26.2) and an NFL-record 6 touchdowns during his career;
- Led the NFL in kickoff-return touchdowns in 1952, 1956, and 1958; in punt-return touchdowns in 1954 and 1955; in punt-return average (18.8) in 1955; and in kickoff-return average (35.5 yards per return) in 1958;
- All-America running back, led the nation in rushing (1,566 yards and 21 touchdowns) as a senior at the University of San Francisco (1951);
- Won a bronze medal in the 400-meter run and a gold medal in the 1,600-meter relay at the 1952 Olympics in Helsinki, Finland. Ran the 100-yard dash in 9.5 seconds.

DEUCE McALLISTER (for more information, see pages 108–109)

| Yr. | Team | G | RUSHING | | | | RECEIVING | | | | TOTAL |
			Att	Yds	Avg	TD	Rec	Yds	Avg	TD	TD
2001	New Orleans	16	16	91	5.7	1	15	166	11.1	1	2
2002	New Orleans	15	325	1,388	4.3	13	47	352	7.5	3	16
Totals		**31**	**341**	**1,479**	**4.3**	**14**	**62**	**518**	**8.4**	**4**	**18**

Transactions
• Selected by New Orleans Saints in the first round (23rd pick overall) of the 2001 NFL Draft.

Noteworthy
• Selected to one Pro Bowl (following the 2002 season);
• Tied Saints single-season record for rushing touchdowns in 2002;
• Led the NFC in rushing yards in 2002;
• Rushed for a career-high 139 yards against San Francisco (Oct. 20, 2002);
• Longest run from scrimmage was 62 yards against Green Bay (Sept. 15, 2002);
• Longest reception was 30 yards against Chicago (Sept. 22, 2002);
• Returned 45 kickoffs for 1,091 yards (24.2-yard average) in 2001;
• Returned 4 punts for 24 yards in 2001;
• Completed 1 of 2 passes for 12 yards and a touchdown;
• Served as student body president during his senior year at Morton High School in Lena, Mississippi.

HUGH McELHENNY (for more information, see pages 84–85)

| YR. | TEAM | G | RUSHING | | | | RECEIVING | | | | TOTAL |
			ATT	YDS	AVG	TD	REC	YDS	AVG	TD	TD
1952	San Francisco	12	98	684	7.0*	6	26	367	14.1	3	10
1953	San Francisco	12	112	503	4.5	3	30	474	15.8	2	5
1954	San Francisco	6	64	515	8.0*	6	8	162	20.3	0	6
1955	San Francisco	12	90	327	3.6	4	11	203	18.5	2	6
1956	San Francisco	12	185	916	5.0	8	16	193	12.1	0	8
1957	San Francisco	12	102	478	4.7	1	37	458	12.4	2	3
1958	San Francisco	12	113	451	4.0	6	31	366	11.8	2	8
1959	San Francisco	10	18	67	3.7	1	22	329	15.0	3	4
1960	San Francisco	9	95	347	3.7	0	14	114	8.1	1	1
1961	Minnesota	13	120	570	4.8	3	37	283	7.6	3	7
1962	Minnesota	11	50	200	4.0	0	16	191	11.9	0	0
1963	N.Y. Giants	14	55	175	3.2	0	11	91	8.3	2	2
1964	Detroit	8	22	48	2.2	0	5	16	3.2	0	0
Totals		**143**	**1,124**	**5,281**	**4.7**	**38**	**264**	**3,247**	**12.3**	**20**	**60**

*Led league

Transactions
- Selected by San Francisco 49ers in first round (ninth pick overall) of the 1952 NFL Draft;
- Selected by Minnesota Vikings in 1961 NFL Expansion Draft;
- Traded by Vikings to New York Giants for fourth-round pick (T Tom Keating) in 1964 NFL Draft and third-round pick (T Archie Sutton) in 1965 draft;
- Signed as a free agent with Detroit Lions in 1964.

Noteworthy
- Inducted into the Pro Football Hall of Fame in 1970;
- Selected to six Pro Bowls (following the 1952, 1953, 1956–58, and 1961 seasons);
- Set NFL records for longest run (89 yards) and longest punt return (94 yards) by a rookie. Both marks have since been broken;
- Member of the 49ers' "Million Dollar Backfield" with quarterback Y.A. Tittle, and fullbacks Joe Perry and John Henry Johnson;
- Had 83 career kickoff returns for 1,921 yards (23.1-yard average) and 126 punt returns for 920 yards (7.3-yard average) and 2 touchdowns;
- His uniform number 39 is retired by the 49ers;
- Set a Pacific Coast Conference rushing mark of 2,499 yards at the University of Washington from 1949–1951;
- Nicknamed "The King."

LENNY MOORE

(for more information, see pages 86–87)

YR.	TEAM	G	RUSHING				RECEIVING				TOTAL
			ATT	YDS	AVG	TD	REC	YDS	AVG	TD	TD
1956	Baltimore	12	86	649	7.5*	8	11	102	9.3	1	9
1957	Baltimore	12	98	458	5.0	3	40	687	17.2	7	11*
1958	Baltimore	12	82	598	7.3*	7	50	938	18.8	7	14
1959	Baltimore	12	92	422	4.6	2	47	846	18.0	6	8
1960	Baltimore	12	91	374	4.1	4	45	936	20.8	9	13
1961	Baltimore	13	92	648	7.0	7	49	728	14.9	8	15
1962	Baltimore	10	106	470	4.4	2	18	215	11.9	2	4
1963	Baltimore	7	27	136	5.0	2	21	288	13.7	2	4
1964	Baltimore	14	157	584	3.7	16*	21	472	22.5	3	20*
1965	Baltimore	12	133	464	3.5	5	27	414	15.3	3	8
1966	Baltimore	13	63	209	3.3	3	21	260	12.4	0	3
1967	Baltimore	14	42	132	3.1	4	13	153	11.8	0	4
Totals		**143**	**1,069**	**5,174**	**4.8**	**63**	**363**	**6,039**	**16.6**	**48**	**111**

*Led league

Transactions
• Selected by Baltimore Colts first round (ninth pick overall) of the 1956 NFL Draft.

Noteworthy
• Inducted into the Pro Football Hall of Fame in 1975;
• Selected to seven Pro Bowls (following the 1956, 1958–1962, and 1964 seasons);
• 1956 NFL rookie of the year;
• Helped Baltimore win two NFL Championship Games (1958 and 1959) and three Western Conference titles (1958, 1959, and 1964);
• Set still-standing NFL record for most consecutive games with a touchdown (18);
• Retired in second place on the NFL's all-time touchdown list;
• Holds Colts records for most points in a season (120 in 1964), career touchdowns and rushing touchdowns, touchdowns and rushing touchdowns in a season, seasons leading the team in touchdowns (6), most career total yards from scrimmage (11,213), seasons with more than 1,000 yards from scrimmage (6), games with more than 100 yards from scrimmage (47), and games with more than 150 yards from scrimmage (16);
• Returned 49 kickoffs for 1,180 yards (24.1-yard average) and a touchdown during his career;
• First player to score 20 touchdowns in a season (1964);
• Recovered a fumble for a touchdown in 1964;
• His uniform number 24 was retired by the Colts;
• Nicknamed the "Reading Rocket" because he was from Reading, Pennsylvania.

MARION MOTLEY (for more information, see pages 60–61)

YR.	TEAM	G	RUSHING				RECEIVING				TOTAL
			ATT	YDS	AVG	TD	REC	YDS	AVG	TD	TD
1946	Cleveland (AAFC)	13	73	601	8.2	5	10	188	18.8	1	6
1947	Cleveland (AAFC)	14	146	889	6.1	8	7	73	10.4	1	10
1948	Cleveland (AAFC)	14	157	964*	6.1	5	13	192	14.8	2	7
1949	Cleveland (AAFC)	11	113	570	5.0	8	15	191	12.7	0	8
1950	Cleveland	12	140	810*	5.8	3	11	151	13.7	1	4
1951	Cleveland	11	61	273	4.5	1	10	52	5.2	0	1
1952	Cleveland	12	104	444	4.3	1	13	213	16.4	2	3
1953	Cleveland	12	32	161	5.0	0	6	47	7.8	0	0
1954			DID NOT PLAY								
1955	Pittsburgh	7	2	8	4.0	0	0	0	—	0	0
AAFC Totals		**52**	**489**	**3,024**	**6.2**	**26**	**45**	**644**	**14.3**	**4**	**31**
NFL Totals		**54**	**339**	**1,696**	**5.0**	**5**	**40**	**463**	**11.6**	**3**	**8**
Totals		**106**	**818**	**4,720**	**44.5**	**31**	**85**	**1,107**	**13.0**	**7**	**39**

*Led league

Transactions

- Signed as a free agent with the Cleveland Browns in the All-America Football Conference (AAFC) in 1946;
- Traded by the Cleveland Browns to the Pittsburgh Steelers for FB Ed Modzelewski (Sept. 15, 1955).

Noteworthy

- Inducted into the Pro Football Hall of Fame in 1968;
- Selected to one Pro Bowl (following the 1950 season);
- While serving in the U.S. Navy, played for future Pro Football Hall of Fame Browns coach Paul Brown at the Great Lakes Naval Training Center in 1945;
- Helped Cleveland win four AAFC championships (1946–49) and one NFL title (1950). Also played in three more NFL Championship Games (1951–53);
- Was the catalyst for one of Paul Brown's most famous innovations—the draw play;
- Set the NFL record by averaging 17.09 yards per carry (188 yards on 11 carries) in a 1950 game against Pittsburgh;
- Also played linebacker and intercepted 2 passes, returning 1 of them 48 yards for a touchdown;
- Is the all-time leading rusher in AAFC history;
- Returned 42 kickoffs for 974 yards (23.2-yard average) for Cleveland in the AAFC;
- He attended McKinley High School in Canton, Ohio—location of the Pro Football Hall of Fame. One other Hall of Fame member, St. Louis Cardinals tackle Dan Dierdorf, also attended high school in Canton.

BRONKO NAGURSKI (for more information, see pages 62–63)

| YR. | TEAM | G | RUSHING | | | | RECEIVING | | | | TOTAL |
			ATT	YDS	AVG	TD	REC	YDS	AVG	TD	TD
1930	Chicago Bears	13	n/a	n/a	n/a	5	n/a	n/a	n/a	0	5
1931	Chicago Bears	10	n/a	n/a	n/a	2	n/a	n/a	n/a	0	2
1932	Chicago Bears	14	121	533	4.4	4*	6	67	11.2	0	4
1933	Chicago Bears	13	128	533	4.2	1	1	23	23.0	0	1
1934	Chicago Bears	13	123	586	4.8	7	3	32	10.7	0	7
1935	Chicago Bears	5	50	170	3.4	1	0	0	0.0	0	1
1936	Chicago Bears	11	122	529	4.3	3	1	12	12.0	0	3
1937	Chicago Bears	10	73	343	4.7	1	0	0	0.0	0	1
1943	Chicago Bears	8	16	84	5.3	1	0	0	0.0	0	1
Totals		**97**	**633**	**2,778**	**4.4**	**25**	**11**	**134**	**12.2**	**0**	**25**

*Led league

Transactions
- Signed as free agent with the Chicago Bears in 1930;
- Signed out of retirement as free agent with Chicago Bears in 1943.

Noteworthy
- Charter enshrinee of the Pro Football Hall of Fame in 1963;
- All-Pro in 1932–34;
- Completed 32 of 77 career NFL pass attempts for 474 yards and 7 touchdowns. Also scored 4 extra points;
- Bears won the 1932 and 1933 NFL titles, and reached the 1934 NFL Championship Game;
- Also played linebacker for the Bears;
- Retired after the 1937 season and became one of the nation's most popular professional wrestlers
- Played running back and tackle for the Bears in 1943 and scored on a 3-yard run to help them defeat the Redskins 41–21 in the NFL Championship Game;
- His uniform number 3 is retired by the Bears;
- All-America at two positions (fullback and tackle) while at the University of Minnesota;
- Given name is Bronislaw.

ERNIE NEVERS (for more information, see pages 44–45)

YR.	TEAM	G	RUSHING				RECEIVING				TOTAL
			ATT	YDS	AVG	TD	REC	YDS	AVG	TD	TD
1926	Duluth	14	n/a	n/a	n/a	8	n/a	n/a	n/a	0	8
1927	Duluth	9	n/a	n/a	n/a	4	n/a	n/a	n/a	0	4
1928			DID NOT PLAY								
1929	Chicago Cardinals	11	n/a	n/a	n/a	12*	n/a	n/a	n/a	0	12*
1930	Chicago Cardinals	11	n/a	n/a	n/a	6	n/a	n/a	n/a	0	6
1931	Chicago Cardinals	9	n/a	n/a	n/a	8	n/a	n/a	n/a	0	8
Totals		**54**	**n/a**	**n/a**	**n/a**	**38**	**n/a**	**n/a**	**n/a**	**0**	**38**

*Led league

Transactions
• Signed as free agent with Duluth Eskimos in 1926;
• Signed as free agent with Chicago Cardinals in 1929.

Noteworthy
• Charter enshrinee of the Pro Football Hall of Fame in 1963;
• Passed for 25 touchdowns and kicked 7 field goals and 52 extra points during his career;
• The Duluth Eskimos also were known as "Ernie Nevers' Traveling Eskimos";
• Holds the NFL record for most points scored in a game with 40 on Thanksgiving Day against the Chicago Bears (Nov. 28, 1929). It is the longest standing individual record in NFL history;
• Played college football for Glenn (Pop) Warner at Stanford University;
• Outperformed Notre Dame's famed Four Horsemen in the 1926 Rose Bowl, although Stanford lost;
• Played baseball for St. Louis Browns of the American League (1926–28);
• Had a 6–12 lifetime pitching record, and gave up 2 of Babe Ruth's record 60 home runs in 1927;
• Got his first major-league hit off Baseball Hall of Fame pitcher Walter Johnson.

WALTER PAYTON (for more information, see pages 20–21)

YR.	TEAM	G	RUSHING ATT	RUSHING YDS	RUSHING AVG	RUSHING TD	RECEIVING REC	RECEIVING YDS	RECEIVING AVG	RECEIVING TD	TOTAL TD
1975	Chicago	13	196	679	3.5	7	33	213	6.5	0	7
1976	Chicago	14	311*	1,390	4.5	13	15	149	9.9	0	13
1977	Chicago	14	339*	1,852*	5.5*	14*	27	269	10.0	2	16*
1978	Chicago	16	333*	1,395	4.2	11	50	480	9.6	0	11
1979	Chicago	16	369*	1,610	4.4	14	31	313	10.1	2	16
1980	Chicago	16	317	1,460	4.6	6	46	367	8.0	1	7
1981	Chicago	16	339	1,222	3.6	6	41	379	9.2	2	8
1982	Chicago	9	148	596	4.0	1	32	311	9.7	0	1
1983	Chicago	16	314	1,421	4.5	6	53	607	11.5	2	8
1984	Chicago	16	381	1,684	4.4	11	45	368	8.2	0	11
1985	Chicago	16	324	1,551	4.8	9	49	483	9.9	2	11
1986	Chicago	16	321	1,333	4.2	8	37	382	10.3	3	11
1987	Chicago	12	146	533	3.7	4	33	217	6.6	1	5
Totals		**190**	**3,838**	**16,726**	**4.4**	**110**	**492**	**4,538**	**9.2**	**15**	**125**

*Led league

Transactions
• Selected by Chicago Bears in first round (fourth pick overall) of the 1975 NFL Draft.

Noteworthy
• Inducted into the Pro Football Hall of Fame in 1993;
• Selected to nine Pro Bowls (following the 1976–1980 and 1983–86 seasons);
• 1977 NFL most valuable player and offensive player of the year;
• Helped the Chicago Bears defeat New England 46–10 in Super Bowl XX;
• Retired as the NFL's all-time leader in rushing yards and touchdowns, 1,000-yard rushing seasons (10), 100-yard rushing games (77), and combined yards from scrimmage (21,264);
• Set an NFL single-game record with 275 rushing yards against Minnesota (Nov. 20, 1977);
• Holds the NFL record for most consecutive starts by a running back (170);
• Holds 28 Bears records;
• Completed 11 of 34 career pass attempts for 331 yards and 8 touchdowns;
• His uniform number 34 is retired by the Bears;
• Rushed for 3,563 yards at Jackson State University and set an NCAA career scoring record with 464 points (66 touchdowns, 5 field goals, and 53 extra points);
• Nickname was "Sweetness";
• The NFL's Man of the Year Award, given annually to the player who defines excellence on and off the field, is named after Payton.

JOE PERRY (for more information, see pages 46–47)

YR.	TEAM	G	ATT	YDS	AVG	TD	REC	YDS	AVG	TD	TOTAL TD
			RUSHING				**RECEIVING**				**TOTAL**
1948	San Fran. (AAFC)	14	77	562	7.3	10	8	79	9.9	1	12
1949	San Fran. (AAFC)	11	115	783	6.8	8	11	146	13.3	3	11
1950	San Francisco	12	124	647	5.2	5	13	69	5.3	1	6
1951	San Francisco	11	136	677	5.0	3	18	167	9.3	1	4
1952	San Francisco	12	158	725	4.6	8	15	81	5.4	0	8
1953	San Francisco	12	192*	1,018*	5.3	10*	19	191	10.1	3	13*
1954	San Francisco	12	173*	1,049*	6.1	8	26	203	7.8	0	8
1955	San Francisco	11	156	701	4.5	2	19	55	2.9	1	3
1956	San Francisco	11	115	520	4.5	3	18	104	5.8	0	3
1957	San Francisco	8	97	454	4.7	3	15	130	8.7	0	3
1958	San Francisco	12	125	758	6.1	4	23	218	9.5	1	5
1959	San Francisco	11	139	602	4.3	3	12	53	4.4	0	3
1960	San Francisco	10	36	95	2.6	1	3	-3	-1.0	0	1
1961	Baltimore	13	168	675	4.0	3	34	322	9.5	1	4
1962	Baltimore	12	94	359	3.8	0	22	194	8.8	0	0
1963	San Francisco	9	24	98	4.1	0	4	12	3.0	0	0
NFL Totals		**156**	**1,737**	**8,378**	**4.8**	**53**	**241**	**1,796**	**7.5**	**8**	**61**
AAFC Totals		**25**	**192**	**1,345**	**7.0**	**18**	**19**	**225**	**11.8**	**4**	**23**
Totals		**181**	**1,929**	**9,723**	**5.0**	**71**	**260**	**2,021**	**7.8**	**12**	**84**

*Led league

Transactions
- Signed as free agent with San Francisco 49ers in the All-America Football Conference (1948);
- Traded by 49ers to Baltimore Colts for 20th-round draft pick (traded) (1961);
- Released by Colts, signed by 49ers (1963).

Noteworthy
- Perry and defensive end Leo Nomellini were the first 49ers inducted into the Pro Football Hall of Fame (1969);
- Selected to three Pro Bowls (following the 1952–54 seasons);
- All-time leading rusher in 49ers history (7,344 yards);
- Ran for more than 100 yards in a game 19 times, a 49ers' record;
- Member of the 49ers' "Million Dollar Backfield" with quarterback Y.A. Tittle, running back Hugh McElhenny, and fullback John Henry Johnson;
- A tremendous athlete, Perry had a kickoff return for a touchdown, intercepted a pass, and made 6 of 7 field-goal attempts during his career;
- His uniform number 34 is retired by the 49ers;
- 49ers discovered Perry while he was playing for the Alameda Naval Air Station. Before that Perry had success at Compton (Calif.) Junior College.

CLINTON PORTIS (for more information, see pages 110–111)

| YR. | TEAM | G | RUSHING | | | | RECEIVING | | | | TOTAL |
			ATT	YDS	AVG	TD	REC	YDS	AVG	TD	TD
2002	Denver	16	273	1,508	5.5	15	33	364	11.0	2	17
Totals		**16**	**273**	**1,508**	**5.5**	**15**	**33**	**364**	**11.0**	**2**	**17**

Transactions
• Selected by Denver Broncos in the second round (51st pick overall) of the 2002 NFL Draft.

Noteworthy
• Named 2002 NFL offensive rookie of the year;
• Led NFL rookies in rushing yards and total yards from scrimmage in 2002;
• Led the NFL in yards per carry among running backs with at least 100 attempts;
• Set club rookie records for most rushing yards in a season and yards per carry;
• Tied a franchise rookie record for rushing touchdowns;
• Set a franchise rookie record for most 100-yard rushing games (8);
• Rushed for a career-high 228 yards against Arizona (Dec. 29, 2002);
• Longest run was 59 yards against Arizona (Dec. 29, 2002);
• Longest reception was a 66-yard touchdown catch against Kansas City (Dec. 15, 2002);
• Helped University of Miami complete undefeated season and defeat Nebraska in the 2001 Rose Bowl to win the 2001 national championship.

JOHN RIGGINS (for more information, see pages 64–65)

YR.	TEAM	G	RUSHING ATT	RUSHING YDS	RUSHING AVG	RUSHING TD	RECEIVING REC	RECEIVING YDS	RECEIVING AVG	RECEIVING TD	TOTAL TD
1971	N.Y. Jets	14	180	769	4.3	1	36	231	6.4	2	3
1972	N.Y. Jets	12	207	944	4.6	7	21	230	11.0	1	8
1973	N.Y. Jets	11	134	482	3.6	4	23	158	6.9	0	4
1974	N.Y. Jets	10	169	680	4.0	5	19	180	9.5	2	7
1975	N.Y. Jets	14	238	1,005	4.2	8	30	363	12.1	1	9
1976	Washington	14	162	572	3.5	3	21	172	8.2	1	4
1977	Washington	5	68	203	3.0	0	7	95	13.6	2	2
1978	Washington	15	248	1,014	4.1	5	31	299	9.6	0	5
1979	Washington	16	260	1,153	4.4	9	28	163	5.8	3	12
1980			DID NOT PLAY								
1981	Washington	15	195	714	3.7	13	6	59	9.8	0	13
1982	Washington	8	177*	553	3.1	3	10	50	5.0	0	3
1983	Washington	15	375	1,347	3.6	24*	5	29	5.8	0	24*
1984	Washington	14	327	1,239	3.8	14*	7	43	6.1	0	14
1985	Washington	12	176	677	3.8	8	6	18	3.0	0	8
Totals		**175**	**2,916**	**11,352**	**3.9**	**104**	**250**	**2,090**	**8.4**	**12**	**116**

*Led league

Transactions
- Selected by N.Y. Jets in first round (sixth pick overall) of the 1971 NFL Draft;
- Signed as free agent with Washington Redskins (June 10, 1976);
- On injured reserve with knee injury (Dec. 6–end of 1977 season);
- Placed on left camp/retired list (July 31, 1980), reactivated (May 25, 1981).

Noteworthy
- Inducted into the Pro Football Hall of Fame in 1992;
- Selected to one Pro Bowl (following the 1975 season);
- 1978 NFL comeback player of the year;
- Ranks tenth on the NFL's all-time rushing list;
- Set then-Super Bowl records for rushing yards (166) and carries (38), scored on a 43-yard touchdown run, and earned game's most-valuable-player honors in Redskins' 27–17 victory over Miami in Super Bowl XVII;
- Had a remarkable four-game stretch in the 1982 postseason, rushing for 610 yards on 136 carries, scoring 4 touchdowns, and accounting for 43 percent of the Redskins' offensive output;
- Set a then-NFL record with 24 rushing touchdowns in 1983;
- Helped Redskins earn berth in Super Bowl XVIII against the Raiders;
- Holds Redskins rushing records for most career yards (7,472), career attempts (1,988), attempts in a season (375 in 1983), career touchdowns (79), touchdowns in a season (24 in 1983), and is tied for most career 100-yard rushing games (19);
- Nickname was "The Diesel."

BARRY SANDERS (for more information, see pages 22–23)

| YR. | TEAM | G | RUSHING | | | | RECEIVING | | | | TOTAL |
			ATT	YDS	AVG	TD	REC	YDS	AVG	TD	TD
1989	Detroit	15	280	1,470	5.3	14	24	282	11.8	0	14
1990	Detroit	16	255	1,304*	5.1	13	36	480	13.3	3	16*
1991	Detroit	15	342	1,548	4.5	16*	41	307	7.5	1	17*
1992	Detroit	16	312	1,352	4.3	9	29	225	7.8	1	10
1993	Detroit	11	243	1,115	4.6	3	36	205	5.7	0	3
1994	Detroit	16	331	1,883*	5.7*	7	44	283	6.4	1	8
1995	Detroit	16	314	1,500	4.8	11	48	398	8.3	1	12
1996	Detroit	16	307	1,533*	5.1	11	24	147	6.1	0	11
1997	Detroit	16	335	2,053*	6.1	11	33	305	9.2	3	14
1998	Detroit	16	343	1,491	4.3	4	37	289	7.8	0	4
Totals		**153**	**3,062**	**15,269**	**5.0**	**99**	**352**	**2,921**	**8.3**	**10**	**109**

*Led league

Transactions
- Selected by Detroit Lions in first round (third pick overall) of 1989 NFL Draft;
- Unexpectedly announced retirement following the 1998 NFL season and only 1,457 yards shy of the league's all-time rushing record.

Noteworthy
- Selected to more Pro Bowls (10) than any other running back in NFL history (following the 1989–1998 seasons);
- 1997 NFL co-most valuable player (shared award with Brett Favre);
- 1994 and 1997 NFL offensive player of the year;
- 1989 NFL rookie of the year;
- Ranks third on the NFL's career rushing list, trailing only Emmitt Smith (17,162 yards) and Walter Payton (16,726);
- Holds the NFL records for most consecutive 100-yard games (14, Sept. 14–Dec. 21, 1997), most games with more than 150 rushing yards (25), and most runs of longer than 50 yards (15);
- Only player in league history to rush for more than 1,500 yards in five seasons and to record two runs of longer than 80 yards in one game. (Sanders had touchdown runs of 80 and 82 yards against Tampa Bay on Oct. 12, 1997.);
- One of only four NFL players to rush for more than 2,000 yards in a season. (O.J. Simpson, 2,003 in 1973; Eric Dickerson, 2,105 in 1984; and Terrell Davis, 2,008 in 1998, are the others.);
- Ran for more than 100 yards in a game 76 times during his career;
- Rushed for a career-high 237 yards against Tampa Bay (Nov. 13, 1994);
- Longest run was 85 yards against Tampa Bay (Oct. 2, 1994);
- Longest reception was a 66-yard touchdown catch against Tampa Bay (Sept. 7, 1997);
- Won Heisman Trophy after rushing for an NCAA-record 2,628 yards and 37 touchdowns during junior season at Oklahoma State in 1988.

GALE SAYERS (for more information, see pages 88–89)

| YR. | TEAM | G | RUSHING | | | | RECEIVING | | | | TOTAL |
			ATT	YDS	AVG	TD	REC	YDS	AVG	TD	TD
1965	Chicago	14	166	867	5.2	14	29	507	17.5	6	22*
1966	Chicago	14	229	1,231*	5.4	8	34	447	13.1	2	12
1967	Chicago	13	186	880	4.7	7	16	126	7.9	1	12
1968	Chicago	9	138	856	6.2*	2	15	117	7.8	0	2
1969	Chicago	14	236*	1,032*	4.4	8	17	116	6.8	0	8
1970	Chicago	2	23	52	2.3	0	1	-6	-6.0	0	0
1971	Chicago	2	13	38	2.9	0	0	0	—	0	0
Totals		**68**	**991**	**4,956**	**5.0**	**39**	**112**	**1,307**	**11.7**	**9**	**56**

*Led league

Transactions
• Selected by Chicago Bears in first round (fourth pick overall) of the 1965 NFL Draft.

Noteworthy
• Inducted into the Pro Football Hall of Fame in 1977;
• Selected to four Pro Bowls (following the 1965–67 and 1969 seasons);
• Led the NFL with 2,272 all-purpose yards and set a then-NFL single-season record of 22 touchdowns (14 rushing, 6 receiving, and 1 each on punt and kickoff returns) as a rookie;
• Holds the NFL rookie record for most touchdowns in a season;
• Is tied with Ernie Nevers and Dub Jones for most touchdowns in a game (6). Scored on an 80-yard pass reception, 21-, 7-, 50-, and 1-yard runs, and an 85-yard punt return against the 49ers (Dec. 12, 1965);
• Returned 91 kickoffs for 2,781 yards (an NFL-record 30.6-yard average) and a league record-tying 6 touchdowns during his career;
• Led the NFL in kickoff-return touchdowns in 1965 (1) and 1966 (2);
• Returned 27 punts for 391 yards (14.5 average) and 2 touchdowns during his career;
• Led the NFL with 1 punt return for a touchdown in 1967;
• Completed 4 of 18 career pass attempts for 111 yards and a touchdown;
• His uniform number 40 is retired by the Bears;
• Had right knee surgery in 1968 and three left knee surgeries in 1970 and 1971;
• Earned nickname "The Kansas Comet" during All-America college career at Kansas.

EMMITT SMITH (for more information, see pages 24–25)

| YR. | TEAM | G | RUSHING | | | | RECEIVING | | | | TOTAL |
			ATT	YDS	AVG	TD	REC	YDS	AVG	TD	TD
1990	Dallas	16	241	937	3.9	11	24	228	9.5	0	11
1991	Dallas	16	365*	1,563*	4.3	12	49	258	5.3	1	13
1992	Dallas	16	373	1,713	4.6	18*	59	335	5.7	1	19*
1993	Dallas	14	283	1,486*	5.3*	9	57	414	7.3	1	10
1994	Dallas	15	368*	1,484	4.0	21*	50	341	6.8	1	22*
1995	Dallas	16	377*	1,773*	4.7	25*	62	375	6.0	0	25*
1996	Dallas	15	327	1,204	3.7	12	47	249	5.3	2	15
1997	Dallas	16	261	1,074	4.1	4	40	234	5.9	0	4
1998	Dallas	16	319	1,332	4.2	13	27	175	6.5	2	15
1999	Dallas	15	329	1,397	4.2	11	27	119	4.4	2	13
2000	Dallas	16	294	1,203	4.1	9	11	79	7.2	0	9
2001	Dallas	14	261	1,021	3.9	3	17	116	6.8	0	3
2002	Dallas	16	254	975	3.8	5	16	89	5.6	0	5
Totals		**201**	**4,052**	**17,162**	**4.2**	**153**	**486**	**3,012**	**6.2**	**11**	**164**

*Led league

Transactions
• Selected by Dallas Cowboys in first round (17th pick overall) of 1990 NFL Draft.

Noteworthy
• Selected to eight Pro Bowls (following the 1990–95, 1998, and 1999 seasons);
• 1993 NFL most valuable player;
• 1990 NFL offensive rookie of the year;
• Helped lead the Cowboys to three Super Bowl victories (XXVII, XXVIII, and XXX), and earned most-valuable-player honors in XXVIII after rushing for 132 yards and 2 touchdowns;
• Became NFL's all-time leading rusher in 2002. Finished the season with 17,162 yards, surpassing Hall of Fame running back Walter Payton (16,726);
• Also holds NFL records for most consecutive seasons and most total seasons with more than 1,000 rushing yards (11), most career rushing touchdowns, and most career rushing attempts;
• Scored an NFL single-season record 25 touchdowns in 1995;
• Holds NFL postseason rushing records for most career yards (1,586), most touchdowns (19), and shares records for most consecutive games with a touchdown (9) and most 100-yard games (7);
• Tied with Bills running back Thurman Thomas for most total touchdowns in postseason history (21);
• Ran for more than 100 yards in a game 76 times during his career, trailing only Walter Payton (77), and tied with Barry Sanders for the second most in NFL history;
• Rushed for a career-high 237 yards against Philadelphia (Oct. 31, 1993);
• Longest run was a 75-yard touchdown against Washington (Sept. 9, 1991);
• Established 58 school records, including most career rushing yards (3,928), at Florida;
• USA Today high school player of the year as senior at Escambia High in Pensacola, Florida.

JIM TAYLOR

(for more information, see pages 66–67)

| YR. | TEAM | G | RUSHING | | | | RECEIVING | | | | TOTAL |
			ATT	YDS	AVG	TD	REC	YDS	AVG	TD	TD
1958	Green Bay	12	52	247	4.8	1	4	72	18.0	1	2
1959	Green Bay	12	120	452	3.8	6	9	71	7.9	2	8
1960	Green Bay	12	230*	1,101	4.8	11	15	121	8.1	0	11
1961	Green Bay	14	243	1,307	5.4	15*	25	175	7.0	1	16*
1962	Green Bay	14	272*	1,474*	5.4	19*	22	106	4.8	0	19*
1963	Green Bay	14	248	1,018	4.1	9	13	68	5.2	1	10
1964	Green Bay	13	235	1,169	5.0	12	38	354	9.3	3	15
1965	Green Bay	13	207	734	3.5	4	20	207	10.4	0	4
1966	Green Bay	14	204	705	3.5	4	41	331	8.1	2	6
1967	New Orleans	14	130	390	3.0	2	38	251	6.6	0	2
Totals		**132**	**1,941**	**8,597**	**4.4**	**83**	**225**	**1,756**	**7.8**	**10**	**93**

*Led league

Transactions
- Selected by Green Bay Packers in second round (15th pick overall) of the 1958 NFL Draft;
- Signed as free agent with New Orleans Saints (1967).

Noteworthy
- Inducted into the Pro Football Hall of Fame in 1976;
- Selected to five Pro Bowls (following the 1960–64 seasons);
- 1962 NFL most valuable player;
- Retired in second place on the NFL's all-time rushing list, trailing only Jim Brown;
- Taylor is the only player to beat out Jim Brown for an NFL rushing title (1962) during Brown's nine-year career;
- Set an NFL record with 19 rushing touchdowns (1962);
- Helped the Packers win four NFL championships (1961, 1962, 1965, and 1966);
- Rushed for 85 yards on 31 carries, with the temperature near zero degrees, in the Packers' 16–7 victory over the New York Giants in the 1962 NFL Championship Game;
- Holds Packers records for most total and rushing touchdowns in a season (19), career rushing yards, rushing yards in a season, career rushing attempts, and 100-yard rushing games (26);
- Returned 7 kickoffs for 185 yards (26.4-yard average) during his career;
- Led the Southeastern Conference in scoring during his junior and senior seasons at Louisiana State University.

THURMAN THOMAS (for more information, see pages 90–91)

			RUSHING				RECEIVING				TOTAL
YR.	TEAM	G	ATT	YDS	AVG	TD	REC	YDS	AVG	TD	TD
1988	Buffalo	15	207	881	4.3	2	18	208	11.6	0	2
1989	Buffalo	16	298	1,244	4.2	6	60	669	11.2	6	12
1990	Buffalo	16	271	1,297	4.8	11	49	532	10.9	2	13
1991	Buffalo	15	288	1,407	4.9*	7	62	631	10.2	5	12
1992	Buffalo	16	312	1,487	4.8	9	58	626	10.8	3	12
1993	Buffalo	16	355*	1,315	3.7	6	48	387	8.1	0	6
1994	Buffalo	15	287	1,093	3.8	7	50	349	7.0	2	9
1995	Buffalo	14	267	1,005	3.8	6	26	220	8.5	2	8
1996	Buffalo	15	281	1,033	3.7	8	26	254	9.8	0	8
1997	Buffalo	16	154	643	4.2	1	30	208	6.9	0	1
1998	Buffalo	14	93	381	4.1	2	26	220	8.5	1	3
1999	Buffalo	5	36	152	4.2	0	3	37	12.3	1	1
2000	Miami	9	28	136	4.9	0	16	117	7.3	1	1
Totals		**182**	**2,877**	**12,074**	**4.2**	**65**	**472**	**4,458**	**9.4**	**23**	**88**

*Led league

Transactions
- Selected by Buffalo Bills in second round (40th pick overall) of the 1988 NFL Draft;
- Released by Bills (Feb. 10, 2000), signed by Miami Dolphins (March 6, 2000);
- On injured reserve with knee injury (Nov. 13–end of 2000 season).

Noteworthy
- Selected to five Pro Bowls (following the 1989–1993 seasons);
- 1991 NFL most valuable player and offensive player of the year;
- Played in four consecutive Super Bowls (XXV, XXVI, XXVII, XXVIII) and five AFC Championship Games (1988 and 1990–93);
- Only player to score a touchdown in four consecutive Super Bowls;
- Holds NFL postseason records for most combined yards gained (2,124) and most consecutive games with a touchdown (9);
- Tied with Emmitt Smith for most total touchdowns (21) and most points scored by a nonkicker (126) in postseason history. Also tied for most receptions (13) in a postseason game;
- Ranks third in postseason history with 339 rushing attempts and 1,442 rushing yards;
- Bills all-time leader in rushing yards and rushing touchdowns;
- Second on the Bills' career reception list, trailing only Andre Reed;
- Ninth on NFL's all-time rushing list and ranks eighth in career 100-yard rushing games (46);
- Rushed for a career-high 214 yards against the N.Y. Jets (Sept. 24, 1990);
- Longest run was an 80-yard touchdown against New England (Nov. 18, 1990);
- Longest reception was a 74-yard touchdown catch against New England (Oct. 1, 1989);
- All-time leading rusher at Oklahoma State University.

JIM THORPE (for more information, see pages 92–93)

| YR. | TEAM | G | RUSHING | | | | RECEIVING | | | | TOTAL |
			ATT	YDS	AVG	TD	REC	YDS	AVG	TD	TD
1920	Canton	9	n/a	n/a	n/a	n/a	n/a	n/a	n/a	n/a	n/a
1921	Cleveland	5	n/a	n/a	n/a	1	n/a	n/a	n/a	n/a	1
1922	Oorang	5	n/a	n/a	n/a	3	n/a	n/a	n/a	n/a	3
1923	Oorang	9	n/a	n/a	n/a	n/a	n/a	n/a	n/a	n/a	n/a
1924	Rock Island	9	n/a	n/a	n/a	n/a	n/a	n/a	n/a	n/a	n/a
1925	New York	3	n/a	n/a	n/a	n/a	n/a	n/a	n/a	n/a	n/a
1925	Rock Island	2	n/a	n/a	n/a	n/a	n/a	n/a	n/a	n/a	n/a
1926	Canton	9	n/a	n/a	n/a	2	n/a	n/a	n/a	n/a	2
1927			DID NOT PLAY								
1928	Chicago Cardinals	1	n/a	n/a	n/a	n/a	n/a	n/a	n/a	n/a	n/a
Totals		**52**	**n/a**	**n/a**	**n/a**	**6**	**n/a**	**n/a**	**n/a**	**n/a**	**6**

Transactions
• Signed as free agent with Canton Bulldogs in 1916;
• Signed as free agent with Cleveland Indians in 1921;
• Signed as free agent with Oorang Indians in 1922;
• Signed as free agent with Rock Island Independents in 1924;
• Signed as free agent with N.Y. Giants and Rock Island Independents in 1925;
• Signed as free agent with Canton Bulldogs in 1926;
• Signed as free agent with Chicago Cardinals in 1928.

Noteworthy
• Charter enshrinee of the Pro Football Hall of Fame in 1963;
• Passed for 4 touchdowns and kicked 4 field goals and 3 extra points during his career;
• In 1950 voted by the nation's sportswriters as the greatest athlete of the first half of the 20th Century;
• Won the pentathlon and decathlon at the 1912 Olympic Games in Sweden;
• Led the Canton Bulldogs to "world championships" in 1916, 1917, and 1919 before the team joined the American Pro Football Association, which later became the NFL;
• Elected as the NFL's first president in 1920;
• Played college football for Glenn (Pop) Warner at Carlisle Indian School;
• Scored NCAA record 198 points as senior (1912);
• Earned five varsity letters in five sports as senior at Carlisle;
• Played Major League Baseball for the New York Giants, Cincinnati Reds, and Boston Braves;
• Was a Sac and Fox Indian, and also had French and Irish ancestry. His tribal name was Wa-Tho-Huk, which means "Bright Path."

LaDainian Tomlinson (for more information, see pages 112–113)

| YR. | TEAM | G | RUSHING | | | | RECEIVING | | | | TOTAL |
			ATT	YDS	AVG	TD	REC	YDS	AVG	TD	TD
2001	San Diego	16	339	1,236	3.6	10	59	367	6.2	0	10
2002	San Diego	16	372	1,683	4.5	14	79	489	6.2	1	15
Totals		**32**	**711**	**2,919**	**4.1**	**24**	**138**	**856**	**6.2**	**1**	**25**

Transactions
- Selected by San Diego Chargers in first round (fifth pick overall) of the 2001 NFL Draft.

Noteworthy
- Selected to one Pro Bowl (following the 2002 season);
- Was the first Chargers running back to make the Pro Bowl since Natrone Means in 1995;
- Named the Chargers' most valuable player in 2002;
- Set or tied eight Chargers records in 2002, including rushing attempts, rushing yards, most receptions by a running back (79), most combined yards (2,172), most rushing yards in a game (220), most 100-yard games (7), and most 200-yard games (2);
- Set Chargers rookie record for rushing yards in a season in 2001;
- Longest run from scrimmage was 76 yards against Denver (Dec. 1, 2002);
- Longest reception was 30 yards against Cincinnati (Sept. 8, 2002);
- All-time leading rusher at the Texas Christian University;
- Only second player in NCAA history to rush for more than 2,000 yards in a season (2,158 in 2000) and 5,000 for a career (5,263);
- Led the nation in rushing in 1999–2000;
- Rushed for an NCAA Divison I single-game record 406 yards against Texas-El Paso in 1999;
- First-team college All-America in 2000 and second-team All-America in 1999;
- Won the Doak Walker Award, given to the nation's best college running back, in 2000.

STEVE VAN BUREN (for more information, see pages 68–69)

| YR. | TEAM | G | RUSHING | | | | | RECEIVING | | | | TOTAL |
			ATT	YDS	AVG	TD	REC	YDS	AVG	TD	TD
1944	Philadelphia	9	80	444	5.6	5	0	0	—	0	7
1945	Philadelphia	10	143	832*	5.8	15*	10	123	12.3	2	18*
1946	Philadelphia	9	116	529	4.6	5	6	75	12.5	0	6
1947	Philadelphia	12	217*	1,008*	4.6	13*	9	79	8.8	0	14*
1948	Philadelphia	11	201*	945*	4.7	10*	10	96	9.6	0	10
1949	Philadelphia	12	263*	1,146*	4.4	11*	4	88	22.0	1	12
1950	Philadelphia	10	188*	629	3.3	4	2	34	17.0	0	4
1951	Philadelphia	10	112	327	2.9	6	4	28	7.0	0	6
NFL Totals		**83**	**1,320**	**5,860**	**4.4**	**69**	**45**	**523**	**11.6**	**3**	**77**

*Led league

Transactions
- Selected by Philadelphia Eagles in first round (fifth pick overall) of the 1944 NFL Draft.

Noteworthy
- Inducted into the Pro Football Hall of Fame in 1965;
- The Pro Bowl was not played from 1943–1949, but Van Buren was selected as a first-team all-league back in 1945 and 1947–49;
- Propelled Philadelphia to three consecutive NFL Championship Games (1947–49);
- Rushed for 98 yards and scored the game's only touchdown in the Eagles' 7–0 victory over the Chicago Cardinals in the 1948 NFL Championship Game;
- Set NFL Championship Game records by setting postseason records with 196 rushing yards on 31 carries in the Eagles' 14–0 victory over the Los Angeles Rams in 1949;
- First NFL player ever to record two 1,000-yard rushing seasons, and both times he set NFL single-season rushing records;
- Led the NFL in rushing, scoring, and kickoff returns in 1947;
- Returned 76 kickoffs for 2,030 yards (26.7-yard average) and 3 touchdowns during his NFL career;
- Led the NFL in kickoff-return average in 1944 (33.3) and 1947 (29.4) and in kickoff returns for touchdowns with 1 in 1944 and 1945;
- Returned 34 punts for 473 yards (13.9 average) and 2 touchdowns during his NFL career;
- Led the NFL in punt returns for touchdowns (1) in 1944 and 1946;
- Also played defensive back for Philadelphia and returned 9 career interceptions for 81 yards. Punted twice for 76 yards (38.0 average);
- His uniform number 15 is retired by the Eagles;
- Born in La Ceiba, Honduras.

RICKY WATTERS (for more information, see pages 48–49)

| YR. | TEAM | G | RUSHING | | | | RECEIVING | | | | TOTAL |
			ATT	YDS	AVG	TD	REC	YDS	AVG	TD	TD
1991	San Francisco	DID NOT PLAY—INJURED									
1992	San Francisco	14	206	1,013	4.9	9	43	405	9.4	2	11
1993	San Francisco	13	208	950	4.6	10	31	326	10.5	1	11
1994	San Francisco	16	239	877	3.7	6	66	719	10.9	5	11
1995	Philadelphia	16	337	1,273	3.8	11	62	434	7.0	1	12
1996	Philadelphia	16	353*	1,411	4.0	13	51	444	8.7	0	13
1997	Philadelphia	16	285	1,110	3.9	7	48	440	9.2	0	7
1998	Seattle	16	319	1,239	3.9	9	52	373	7.2	0	9
1999	Seattle	16	325	1,210	3.7	5	40	387	9.7	2	7
2000	Seattle	16	278	1,242	4.5	7	63	613	9.7	2	9
2001	Seattle	5	72	318	4.4	1	11	107	9.7	0	1
Totals		**144**	**2,622**	**10,643**	**4.1**	**78**	**467**	**4,248**	**9.1**	**13**	**91**

*Led league

Transactions
- Selected by San Francisco 49ers in second round (45th pick overall) of 1991 NFL Draft;
- On injured reserve with foot injury (Aug. 27–end of 1991 season);
- Granted restricted free agency, signed by the Philadelphia Eagles (March 18, 1995);
- Granted unconditional free agency, signed by the Seattle Seahawks (March 4, 1998).

Noteworthy
- Selected to five Pro Bowls (following the 1992–96 seasons);
- Only player in NFL history to rush for more than 1,000 yards in a season for three different teams;
- Set NFL postseason single-game records for most points (30), touchdowns (5), and rushing touchdowns (5) in a divisional playoff game against the New York Giants (Jan. 15, 1994);
- Scored 3 touchdowns in the 49ers' 49–26 victory over the San Diego Chargers in Super Bowl XXIX and is tied with Roger Craig (XIX), Jerry Rice (XXIV), and Terrell Davis (XXXII) for the Super Bowl single-game record of most touchdowns in a game;
- All four players also hold the record for most points (18) in a Super Bowl;
- Ranks twelfth on the league's all-time rushing list;
- Ran for more than 100 yards in a game 32 times during his career;
- Rushed for a career-high 178 yards against Indianapolis (Dec. 20, 1998);
- Longest run was 57 yards against the New York Giants (Nov. 19, 1995);
- Longest reception was a 65-yard touchdown catch against Denver (Dec. 17, 1994);
- Completed 1 of 2 career pass attempts for 1 yard and a touchdown;
- Played flanker for the University of Notre Dame in 1988 and caught a team-high 15 passes for 286 yards and 2 touchdowns to help the Fighting Irish win the national championship.

RICKY WILLIAMS (for more information, see pages 114–115)

| YR. | TEAM | G | RUSHING | | | | RECEIVING | | | | TOTAL |
			ATT	YDS	AVG	TD	REC	YDS	AVG	TD	TD
1999	New Orleans	12	253	884	3.5	2	28	172	6.1	0	2
2000	New Orleans	10	248	1,000	4.0	8	44	409	9.3	1	9
2001	New Orleans	16	313	1,245	4.0	6	60	511	8.5	1	7
2002	Miami	16	383	1,853*	4.8	16	47	363	7.7	1	17
Totals		**54**	**1,197**	**4,982**	**4.2**	**32**	**179**	**1,455**	**8.1**	**3**	**35**

*Led league

Transactions
- Selected by New Orleans Saints in first round (fifth pick overall) of the 1999 NFL Draft;
- Traded with a fourth-round choice (TE Randy McMichael) in the 2002 NFL Draft by the Saints to the Miami Dolphins for first- (DE Charles Grant) and fourth-round (CB Keyuo Craver) choices in the 2002 draft and a third-round choice in the 2003 draft.

Noteworthy
- New Orleans traded all of its selections in 1999 NFL draft and first- and third-round choices in 2000 draft to move up and select Williams with fifth overall choice in 1999 draft;
- Selected to one Pro Bowl (following the 2002 season);
- Led the NFL in rushing in 2002;
- Set Miami single-season rushing records for attempts, yards, most 100-yard games (10), and touchdowns in 2002;
- Also set Miami single-season record for total touchdowns in 2002 and set record for most yards in a game with a career-high 228 against Buffalo (Dec. 1, 2002);
- Longest run from scrimmage was a 63-yard touchdown against Chicago (Dec. 9, 2002);
- Longest reception was 52 yards against Indianapolis (Sept. 15, 2002);
- Completed 1 of 2 career passes for 34 yards;
- Held 20 NCAA rushing records—including most career rushing yards (6,279), all-purpose yards (7,206), highest yard-per-carry average (6.2), rushing touchdowns (72), and total touchdowns (75)—when he finished college career at the University of Texas;
- Won the Heisman Trophy, Maxwell Award, and Walter Camp Award as the nation's best college player after rushing for 2,124 yards his senior year at Texas in 1998;
- First player to win the Doak Walker Award, as the nation's best college running back, in consecutive seasons (1997 and 1998);
- Set 44 school records at Texas;
- Selected by the Philadelphia Phillies in the eighth round of the 1995 Major League Baseball Draft. Part of the Phillies', Montreal Expos', and Texas Rangers' minor-league systems during his four-year (1995–98) career.

PHOTO CREDITS

Cover Peter Brouillet
1 Al Messerschmidt
2 Dickerson: John McDonough
   Dorsett: Jonathan Daniel
3 Rob Brown
6–7 Glenn James
8 John E. Biever
9 Rob Brown
10 Tony Tomsic
11 Tony Tomsic
12 Michael Zagaris
13 John McDonough
14 Jonathan Daniel
15 Allan Kaye
16 Paul Jasienski
17 Peter Brouillet
18 George Gojkovich
19 Bill Smith
20 Al Messerschmidt
21 Paul Jasienski
22 Robert Skeoch
23 Bob Rosato
24 James D. Smith
25 Glenn James
26–27 Marty Morrow
28 Allen Kee
29 Ralph Waclawicz
30 Greg Trott
31 Michael Zagaris
32 Joe Poellot
33 Bob Rosato
34 Paul Jasienski
35 Matthew Emmons
36 John E. Biever
37 Manny Rubio
38 Marty Morrow
39 Paul Jasienski

40 Tony Tomsic
41 Tony Tomsic
42 Scott Boehm
43 David Drapkin
44 Pro Football HOF
45 Pro Football HOF
46 Pro Football HOF
47 Frank Rippon
48 Michael Zagaris
49 Mickey Pfleger
50–51 Sylvia Allen
52 Paul Jasienski
53 Allen Kee
54 Lou Witt
55 Manny Rubio
56 Sylvia Allen
57 Malcolm Emmons
58 Laughead Photographers
59 Malcolm Emmons
60 Pro Football HOF
61 Frank Kuchirchuk
62 Pro Football HOF
63 Pro Football HOF
64 Ron Ross
65 Tony Tomsic
66 David Boss
67 Robert Riger
68 Nate Fine
69 Philadelphia Eagles
70–71 Vernon Biever
72 Mitchell B. Reibel
73 David Drapkin
74 G. Newman Lowrance
75 Paul Jasienski
76 NFL Photos
77 NFL Photos
78 Vernon Biever

79 Tony Tomsic
80 George Rose
81 Peter Brouillet
82 Russ Reed
83 Vic Stein
84 Pro Football HOF
85 Frank Rippon
86 Darryl Norenberg
87 NFL Photos
88 Vernon Biever
89 Malcolm W. Emmons
90 Louis A. Raynor
91 Bob Rosato
92 Pro Football HOF
93 Pro Football HOF
94–95 Allen Kee
96 Tami Tomsic
97 Tami Tomsic
98 Vincent Manniello
99 James Biever
100 J. Schwaberow/Clarkson
101 George Gojkovich
102 NFLP/G. Newman Lowrance
103 Tracy Frankel
104 Allen Kee
105 Evan Pinkus
106 George Gojkovich
107 Paul Jasienski
108 Joe Robbins
109 Vincent Muzik
110 J. Schwaberow/Clarkson
111 NFLP/Joseph Poellot
112 Aggie Skirball
113 G. Newman Lowrance
114 Scott Boehm
115 Allen Kee
116–117 Tony Tomsic

SOURCES

Statistical information was provided by various sources, including *Total Football II* and the *2003 NFL Record & Fact Book*.

ABOUT THE AUTHOR

Brian Peterson is a Senior Editor for NFL Creative, based in Los Angeles.